MW01592389

# CAMOUFLAGE
# SIMPLIFIED

### By ERIC SLOANE

**author of**
**CLOUDS, AIR & WIND**

THE DEVIN-ADAIR COMPANY · Publishers

NEW YORK · 1942

**FIRST EDITION • COPYRIGHT 1942 BY ERIC SLOANE**

All rights reserved. Permission to reproduce material from this book must
be obtained in writing from the Devin-Adair Co., 23 East 26 Street, N. Y.
Printed in the United States of America by Burr Printing House, Inc.

**TYPOGRAPHY BY LEWIS F. WHITE**

A PATHFINDER BOOKS REPRINT EDITION
Printed in the United States of America
ISBN-13: 978-1523668854
ISBN-10: 1523668857

# CONTENTS

# AUTHOR'S NOTE

Shortly after Pearl Harbor, the thought of camouflage began to appear in the minds of a number of persons concerned with the handling of vital materials.

Nearly twenty-five years had elapsed since most of us had thought much of this word, long associated in our minds with the elaborate dazzle-patterns of the first World War. Had aerial photography and the modern high flying bomber altered the problem this time, and were different techniques in order? It would seem so.

Many architectural and engineering firms were confronted with bids for concealing defense factories at the outbreak of war and Mr. H. G. Matthews of the Engineering firm of Brown & Matthews, asked me to look into modern camouflage for him and report my findings for the reference library of his staff of engineers. That is how this book came to be done. It is not an official authority nor does it reflect the opinions of anyone but myself; I compiled it mainly as a personal record of my own experiments in the hope of simplifying theories of concealment for the average interested person.

I am particularly indebted to Major Peter Rod-yenko, U. S. A., for his valuable assistance and for making his extensive material available to me especially on the subject of the aerial camera.

ERIC SLOANE

# INTRODUCTION

This book contains no military secrets. It is a collection of notes of the most elementary nature compiled with the intention of simplifying in the reader's mind the meaning of camouflage.

This science frequently has been misinterpreted as a secret branch of art designed to trick an enemy with fantastic designs and optical illusions; actually it is a sound study of protective concealment. In order to understand the theory of concealment, we must differentiate at once between these outlandish, scattered, hit or miss schemes—often poorly devised and of little or no actual value—and the true science of camouflage.

The best proving ground for camouflage is of course an area under attack and it is well to remember that in total warfare no distinction is made between areas allotted to armed forces, military works, the civilian population, or civilian industrial establishments. For this reason, it seems fairly important that every citizen should have at least some appreciation of the exactitude and limitations of the science. New methods of detecting camouflage such as the infra-red camera, the stereoscope, the various highly sensitized films, plus the simultaneous development of new methods of outwitting these inventions, make the work doubly interesting and can often take on the aspects of a game.

They tell of an airport in England designed to appear from aloft like a village, where visiting pilots are instructed to make their approach along the main street, set down upon the village square and taxi immediately into the city hall. Another tale concerns a fake airport which was bombed by fake wooden bombs in an attempt to ridicule the poor camouflage efforts displayed there. Stories like these, building up the romantic and humorous side of camouflage tend to give an erroneous impression, for good concealment calls for hard work, much structural labor and plenty of good plain horse sense.

Fig. 1

Optical illusions seem easy to create when done on drawing boards and with paper models. Transferred to real life, elements such as weather, season, moving shadow, sunlight, and structural difficulties enter the picture accordingly. Models and sketches should be considered only after the research-photographer and the camouflage-engineer have had a chance to consider the problem from all its angles, emphasizing of course the most important angle of all—the air.

(Fig. 1) presents a typical problem. It might at first seem a good plan for the industrial plant shown, since it is situated among scattered sandpits, to disguise itself as a sandpit (A). But real sandpits fill with water and snow while the artificial ones never do. Notice too, how this sandpit design actually makes a target of the factory instead of concealing it. Now see how a disrupting plan (B) would make it *less* conspicuous. A "roadway" has been continued over the roof while an artificial sandpit has been introduced away from the center of the building.

Perhaps the peacetime architect of the future will incorporate the concealment factor in his industrial plans, and thereby make conversion simpler and less costly when war comes. But for the present, those of us who participate in blackouts and similar defensive measures should know something about the theory of concealment. Improper or ill-conceived camouflage can be worse than none at all. (Fig. 2)

Fig. 2

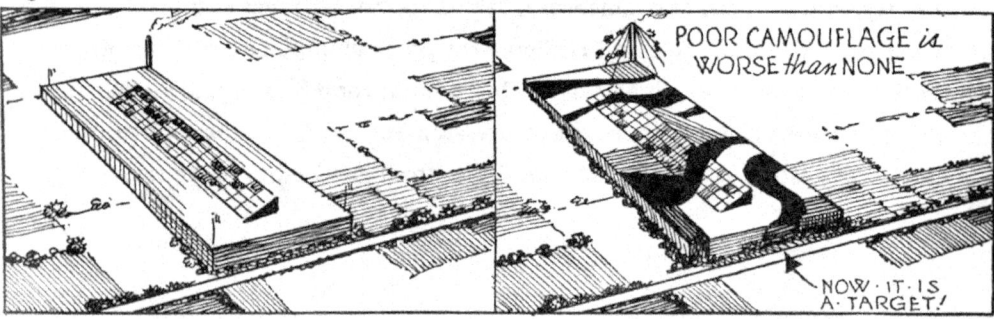

POOR CAMOUFLAGE *is* WORSE *than* NONE

NOW · IT · IS A · TARGET!

# I

Camouflage means disguise; disguise is one of the first forms of protection in combat. The first elaborate examples of camouflage, like many another first attempt, were much overdone especially as to color and design. The practice has now settled down to one of practical protective concealment without artistic trickery. The camoufleur has had to abandon his palette and smock and now looks more like an Army man with an engineering background.

The science of concealment is not new—it is a natural impulse for both the attacker and the attacked. We are acquainted with the pygmy hunter approaching a zebra-herd wearing a zebra-like costume, the duck hunter using decoys, the American Indian dressed to blend with the forest; all are practicing sound camouflage. And of course, there is that great example of successful camouflage, the famous Trojan Horse.

Camouflage is divided into two branches, one of actual concealment and one of confusion. If a factory can be concealed it is more difficult to bomb. If bombing is inevitable, a fake factory may be made in mimicry to draw the bombs, sparing the real one, or causing misses in the confusion.

*Camouflage then, is that science of disguise by which we may conceal ourselves from attack, or lessen our vulnerability when attacked or attacking.* First World War camouflage dealt mostly with ground attack; now attack comes chiefly from the air and unless we are familiar with our subject from aloft, especially through the camera's eye, we are not capable of designing good camouflage.

Whether to camouflage or not depends upon many factors. Modern attack planes do not go out like marauders in search of likely places to drop bombs; they are sent upon definite missions to destroy definite objectives that have first been photographed and studied from high altitudes. Of course, if the objective is concealed or the bombers are intercepted, they will drop their load of bombs upon the next best target and streak for home. But the day of the individual fighter is gone and bombing is done with foresight, every detail planned in advance.

It is logical then, that to start research for concealment plans, extensive observations—ground and aerial—must be made at different hours of the day and night. It is imperative to make a study of aerial photographs of the area in which operations are planned. The average distance from which a target can be recognized varies between four and six miles, this estimate being for high flying bombers and photographers. The camoufleur must note from these distances, the shadows, reflections, smoke, roadways, colorations and landmarks that serve to define the object to be concealed not only to the naked eye but to the camera as well. The first step in planning a concealment program then is to put one's self in the place of an enemy observer looking for evidences of human activity.

New plants should be definitely planned with camouflage and defense features built in. In Germany for instance, no new industrial buildings may be erected without concealment plans having been made and passed by the government. One or two story buildings cast less shadow than taller buildings. Instead of crowding a factory into one large building, a number of smaller buildings might better be placed irregularly and landscaped with trees in order to run less risk of disrupting an entire industry when bombs come. Interior lighting and air conditioning should replace the large glass partitions and skylights ordinarily used. Tall chimneys which are constructed to create a draft, should be cut short and a forced draft introduced. Covering a beautiful new white tile building with tar emulsion, wires, nets, rags and other material *after completion* can be very disheartening to the owner, who may balk at the expense involved and doubt the value of hiding his million dollar factory with a half million dollars worth of seemingly weird drapings. It may take an actual bombing to make him change his mind. (Fig. 3)

Fig. 3

BEFORE

AFTER

$ 1,000,000.⁰⁰

$ 1,500,000.⁰⁰

# AERIAL OBSERVATION
## 2

We have noted that modern total warfare makes no distinction between civilian and industrial areas and areas devoted to military establishments and forces; and it is the hostile observation plane flying over these several areas, equipped with every means for visual and photographic detection, which is the precise weapon the camoufleur must outwit. In order to do this successfully, he must use aerial observation and photography in planning, applying and evaluating the effectiveness of his camouflage.

The development of aerial photography since the Armistice has been tremendous, and aerial photographs are now used extensively by most civilian business as well as by army authorities. The advantage of these photographs is not only that they show the ground exactly and in detail, but also that they give the actual present condition of objects on the ground which is rarely the case with maps.

Several types of aerial photographs are used: Verticals which show large areas and pick up all shadows; Pinpoints which display a particular object in detail; Mosaics which are valuable for study of large areas of surrounding terrain; and Obliques which give the panoramic view. But for our purpose, the two types of greatest interest to the camoufleur are the Stereograph, and the picture developed from the infra-red ray film.

The Stereoscope or two-eyed camera takes a picture showing objects in three dimensions, and this camera is difficult to fool. For this reason, in areas important enough to tempt stereoscopic detection, it is wise to construct all "dummies" of surrounding material and to build them as realistically as possible. For instance, artificial trees should always match surrounding foliage and be of the type grown in the particular neighborhood. The human eye is easy to deceive; the camera somewhat harder; but the Stereoscope is the detective of camouflage.

The infra-red ray photograph is used to detect camouflage by comparing its artificial material and coloration with surrounding natural vegetation. Most common colored paints reflect infra-red as though they were white or nearly white, thereby making it obvious to an observer that the camoufleur has been at work. However, special infra-red paints which will not change in values when infra-red photographed are now available on the market and these considerably neutralize the use of this film. In the following pages when "paint" is mentioned, it is to be assumed that these infra-red paints are to be used unless otherwise indicated.

Evidences of human activity are another factor shown on the aerial photograph with relentless clarity. The most perfect camouflage installation is of no use at all if workers will not confine themselves and their machines to the roadways, and entrances and exits planned for them. It is not impossible that one tire track glaringly out of place in a photograph may bring on devastation; but strange as it seems, one of the camoufleur's most difficult jobs is getting this fact across to the human beings in question.

This struggle between observation versus camouflage is in reality like a tug-of-war; it is never static and keeps shifting from one side to the other. New facilities for observation have been and will be invented, and new methods for defeating these facilities have been and will be found by the camouflage expert. That he can and will defeat them depends not only upon his knowledge, cleverness and ingenuity; but also upon the cooperation and assistance given him by the people he is working to protect.

# PRELIMINARY CONCEALMENT

## 3

Camouflage is only one element in the protection of an industrial plant in wartime. In (Fig. 4) fifteen important defensive measures are indicated. An enemy attacker affects each item from 1 to 15 and in this general order, but the defender should start his defense preparations in the opposite order, or from 15 to 1. Actual camouflage then should be the final step in a defense program rather than the first step.

Protective concealment for War Dept. sponsored industries has been placed in charge of the Chief of Engineers U.S.A. who operates through his District Engineer Offices. When the question of camouflage arises, the proper military authorities should be consulted.

Elementary precautions such as blackout preparation, shelters, reflection elimination, and other details can be taken care of in advance, but it might be wise first to determine the extent of final concealment so that none of this elementary work need be canceled or remade. For example, a smokestack camouflaged with costly wires and nets may later have to be eliminated entirely and a forced draft installed. Or again, blackout curtains may be installed in a plant and later a shatterproof covering which also acts as a blackout may be decided upon, making the curtains useless.

Fig. 4

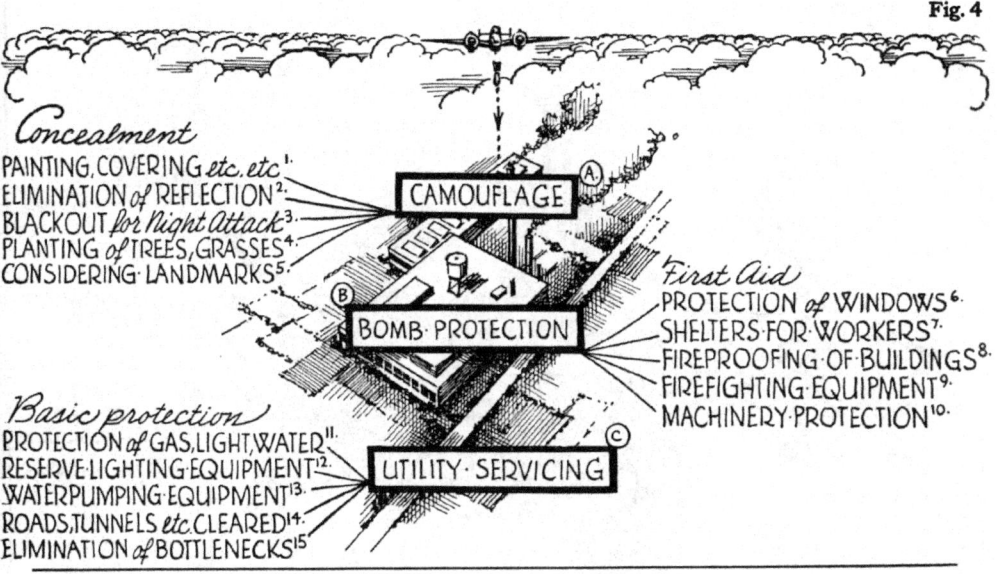

*Concealment*
PAINTING, COVERING *etc. etc.*[1]
ELIMINATION *of* REFLECTION[2]
BLACKOUT *for Night Attack*[3]
PLANTING *of* TREES, GRASSES[4]
CONSIDERING LANDMARKS[5]

CAMOUFLAGE Ⓐ

*First Aid*
PROTECTION *of* WINDOWS[6]
SHELTERS FOR WORKERS[7]
FIREPROOFING OF BUILDINGS[8]
FIREFIGHTING EQUIPMENT[9]
MACHINERY PROTECTION[10]

Ⓑ BOMB PROTECTION

*Basic protection*
PROTECTION *of* GAS, LIGHT, WATER[11]
RESERVE LIGHTING EQUIPMENT[12]
WATERPUMPING EQUIPMENT[13]
ROADS, TUNNELS *etc.* CLEARED[14]
ELIMINATION *of* BOTTLENECKS[15]

Ⓒ UTILITY SERVICING

15

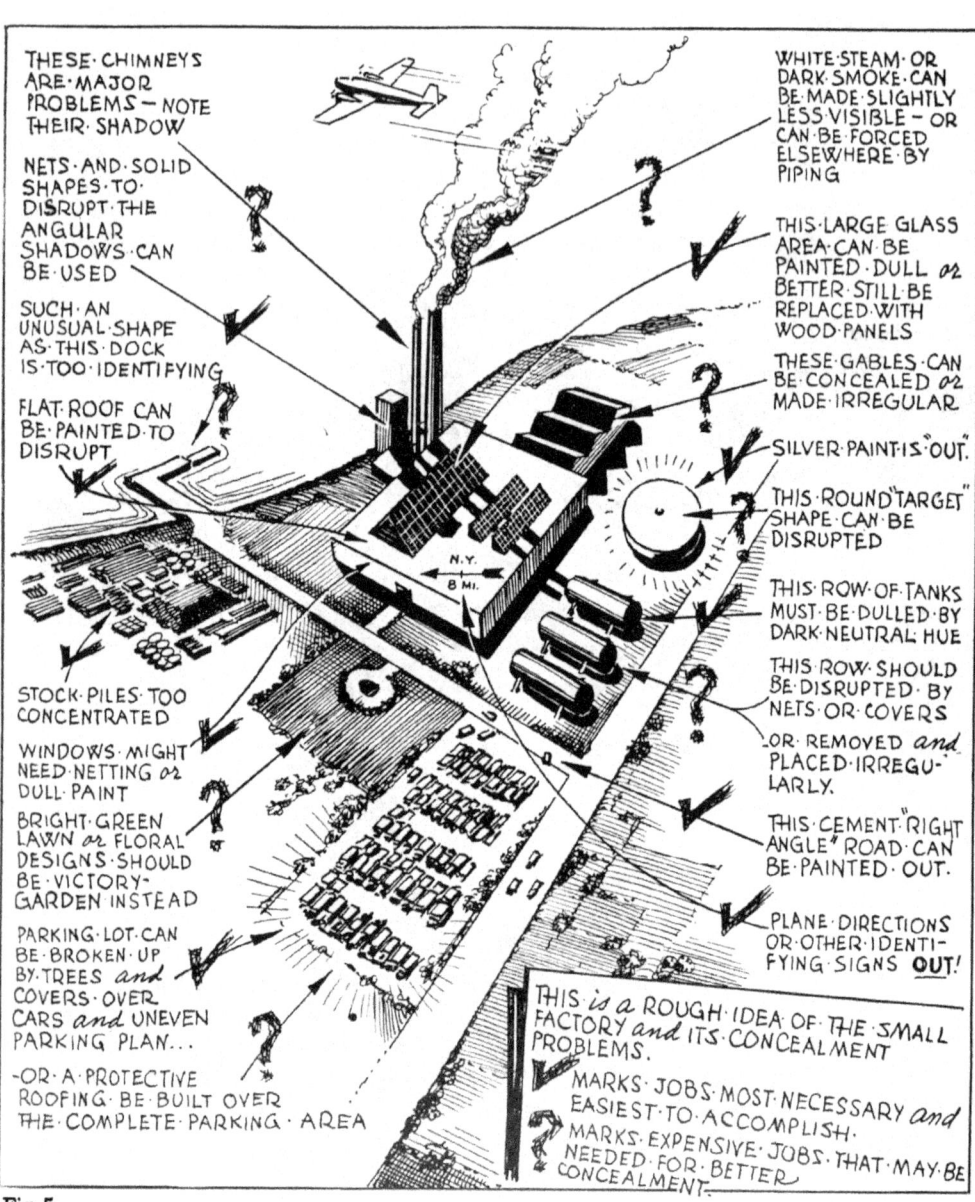

THESE CHIMNEYS ARE MAJOR PROBLEMS — NOTE THEIR SHADOW

NETS AND SOLID SHAPES TO DISRUPT THE ANGULAR SHADOWS CAN BE USED

SUCH AN UNUSUAL SHAPE AS THIS DOCK IS TOO IDENTIFYING

FLAT ROOF CAN BE PAINTED TO DISRUPT

STOCK PILES TOO CONCENTRATED

WINDOWS MIGHT NEED NETTING or DULL PAINT

BRIGHT GREEN LAWN or FLORAL DESIGNS SHOULD BE VICTORY-GARDEN INSTEAD

PARKING LOT CAN BE BROKEN UP BY TREES and COVERS OVER CARS and UNEVEN PARKING PLAN...

—OR A PROTECTIVE ROOFING BE BUILT OVER THE COMPLETE PARKING AREA

WHITE STEAM OR DARK SMOKE CAN BE MADE SLIGHTLY LESS VISIBLE — OR CAN BE FORCED ELSEWHERE BY PIPING

THIS LARGE GLASS AREA CAN BE PAINTED DULL or BETTER STILL BE REPLACED WITH WOOD PANELS

THESE GABLES CAN BE CONCEALED or MADE IRREGULAR

SILVER PAINT IS "OUT"

THIS ROUND "TARGET" SHAPE CAN BE DISRUPTED

THIS ROW OF TANKS MUST BE DULLED BY DARK NEUTRAL HUE

THIS ROW SHOULD BE DISRUPTED BY NETS OR COVERS

OR REMOVED and PLACED IRREGULARLY.

THIS CEMENT "RIGHT ANGLE" ROAD CAN BE PAINTED OUT.

PLANE DIRECTIONS OR OTHER IDENTIFYING SIGNS **OUT**!

N.Y. 8 MI.

THIS is a ROUGH IDEA OF THE SMALL FACTORY and ITS CONCEALMENT PROBLEMS.

MARKS JOBS MOST NECESSARY and EASIEST TO ACCOMPLISH.

MARKS EXPENSIVE JOBS THAT MAY BE NEEDED FOR BETTER CONCEALMENT.

Fig. 5

(Fig. 5) is intended to show a few of the more important concealment principles of use to the average small factory. Note the features that an attacker would spot: The sharp gable shadows, the round tank, the three tanks in a row, the parking space, the dock, the smoke, the bright green lawn.

Inasmuch as this factory might be part of a greater camouflage scheme however, no one but military authorities could recommend actual concealment treatment.

# CONCEALMENT IN NATURE

## 4

As we have noted, camouflage is divided into concealment and confusion (or disruption). Nature uses these two methods to good effect. The bat is camouflaged for simple concealment. Lacking dazzle design or confusing pattern, it garbs itself in dull black to blend with the night scene. Toads, insects and many animals are also designed to match their surroundings, but many species which travel away from their natural habitats have their coloration painted upon them in a disruptive design. This does not hide them in an exposed habitat but it does help to make them look like something they are not. For instance, consider the frog in (A) (Fig. 6). He is colored to match the grass that usually protects him, but should he sit upon a rock (B) his design would cause him to assume a shape other than a frog shape. A hawk constantly on the lookout for a frog shape will fly about until that shape is duplicated in his vision, but the disruptive pattern has created an illusion of a different shape, and he will not readily spot the frog.

Some animals hug the ground when attacking, an attitude that causes the least ground shadow. Butterflies when at rest often fold their wings toward the sun, casting almost no shadow upon the ground to betray their presence. Shadow is important, one of the greatest obstacles to be overcome in military camouflage as we shall see.

The application of disruptive design is accomplished by coloration, shadow, outline and many ways particularly interesting to the camoufleur.

Fig. 6

A pure white animal standing against a white wall would not *appear* all white in sunlight. The shaded under-parts would look black. To get around this nature uses countershadow. This is simply lightening shaded portions and darkening upper, sunlit portions. (Fig. 7). Some of nature's countershadowings are masterpieces of blending.

Caterpillars protect themselves by countershading. Their dark dull backs absorb light rays, while their lighter underparts serve to paint out both shadows and highlights. Countershading is most effective from a side or horizontal view so that its application in camouflage is not against overhead

Fig. 7

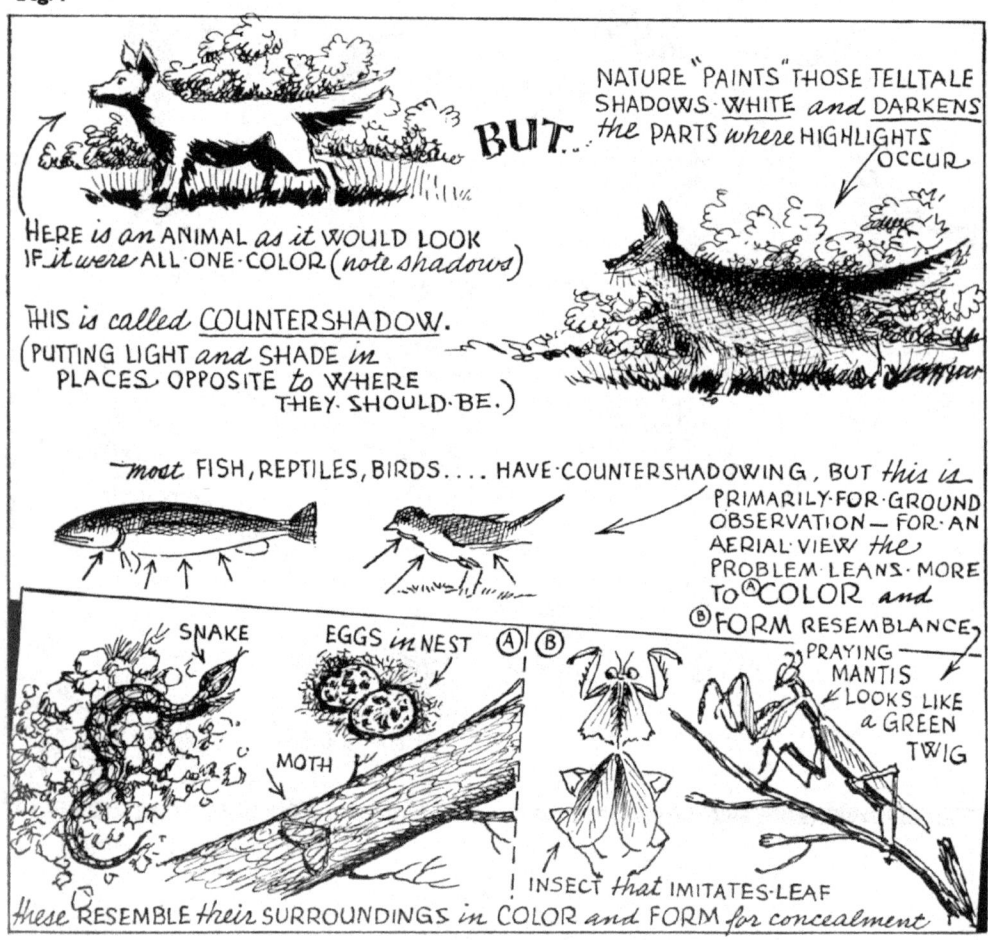

HERE *is an* ANIMAL *as it* WOULD LOOK IF *it were* ALL·ONE·COLOR (*note shadows*)

THIS *is called* COUNTERSHADOW. (PUTTING LIGHT *and* SHADE *in* PLACES OPPOSITE *to* WHERE THEY·SHOULD·BE.)

BUT... NATURE "PAINTS" THOSE TELLTALE SHADOWS·WHITE *and* DARKENS *the* PARTS *where* HIGHLIGHTS OCCUR

*most* FISH, REPTILES, BIRDS.... HAVE·COUNTERSHADOWING, BUT *this is* PRIMARILY·FOR·GROUND OBSERVATION — FOR·AN AERIAL·VIEW *the* PROBLEM·LEANS·MORE TO ⓐCOLOR *and* ⓑFORM RESEMBLANCE

SNAKE    EGGS *in* NEST  Ⓐ Ⓑ    PRAYING MANTIS LOOKS LIKE *a* GREEN TWIG

MOTH

INSECT *that* IMITATES·LEAF

*these* RESEMBLE *their* SURROUNDINGS *in* COLOR *and* FORM *for concealment*

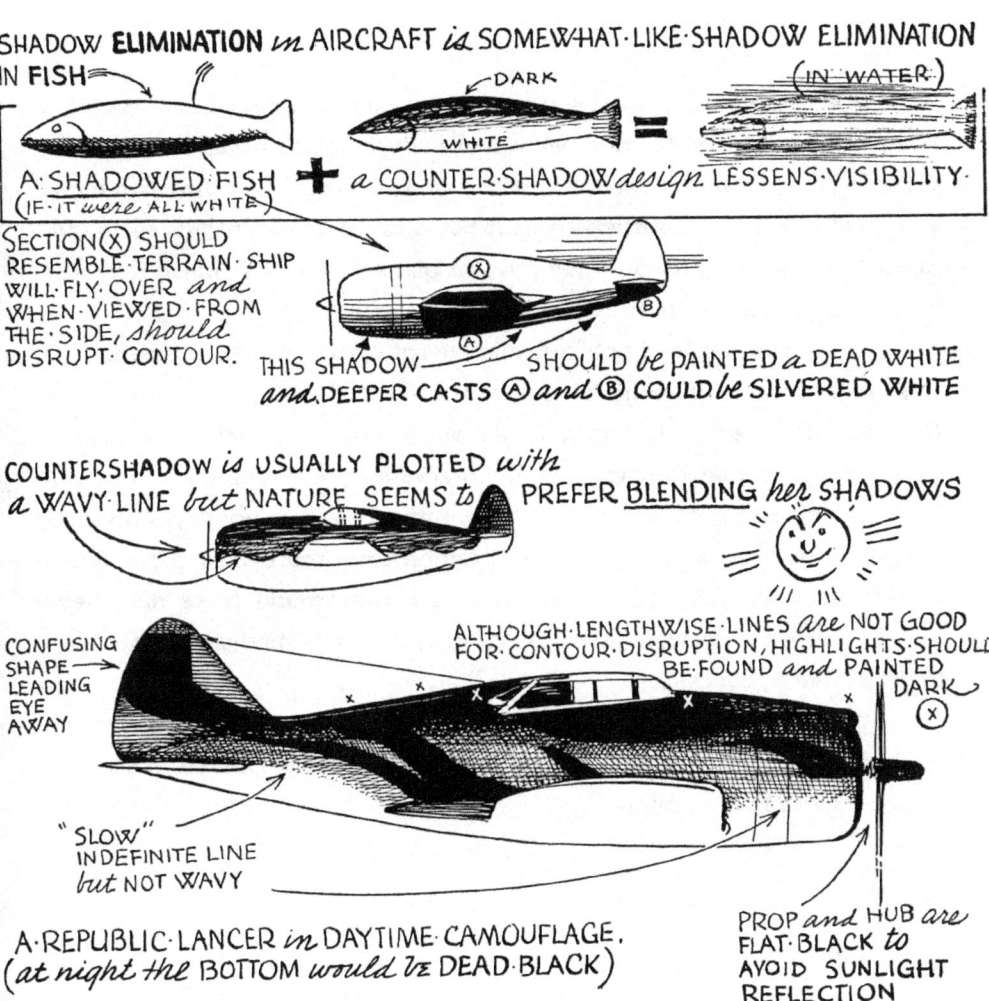

SHADOW **ELIMINATION** *in* AIRCRAFT *is* SOMEWHAT·LIKE·SHADOW ELIMINATION IN FISH

DARK

WHITE

(IN·WATER·)

A·SHADOWED·FISH (IF·IT *were* ALL·WHITE) **+** *a* COUNTER·SHADOW *design* LESSENS·VISIBILITY·

SECTION (X) SHOULD RESEMBLE·TERRAIN·SHIP WILL·FLY·OVER *and* WHEN·VIEWED·FROM THE·SIDE, *should* DISRUPT·CONTOUR.

THIS SHADOW——— SHOULD *be* PAINTED *a* DEAD WHITE *and*.DEEPER CASTS Ⓐ *and* Ⓑ COULD *be* SILVERED WHITE

COUNTERSHADOW *is* USUALLY PLOTTED *with* *a* WAVY·LINE *but* NATURE SEEMS *to* PREFER BLENDING *her* SHADOWS

CONFUSING SHAPE → LEADING EYE AWAY

ALTHOUGH·LENGTHWISE·LINES *are* NOT GOOD FOR·CONTOUR·DISRUPTION,HIGHLIGHTS·SHOULD BE·FOUND *and* PAINTED DARK (X)

"SLOW" INDEFINITE LINE *but* NOT WAVY

A·REPUBLIC·LANCER *in* DAYTIME·CAMOUFLAGE. (*at night the* BOTTOM *would be* DEAD·BLACK)

PROP *and* HUB *are* FLAT·BLACK *to* AVOID SUNLIGHT REFLECTION

Fig. 8

attack. Consequently it is of minor importance in industrial plant protection.

(Fig. 8) shows the countershading of a fish adapted to the airplane fuselage. Since an attacking airplane is rarely viewed from the side except by another plane, when concealment is impossible, most effort is directed toward the plane's upper surfaces where color-resemblance is applied.

Just as the white animal will not appear white because of its shadows, a white airplane as viewed from below looks anything but white. Only when a plane is flying in sunlight and can reflect some of the glare of the earth by its white belly and under-surfaces does it begin to disappear into its surroundings. On even a slightly dull day a white plane will appear black from the ground for we can see only its shaded portion.

Another example of nature's methods, of interest to the camoufleur, is form resemblance, or mimicry. Insects that look like twigs or leaves, birds that resemble reeds, fish that look like weeds, are all mimicking something they are not, so that they may avoid observation by enemies. Mimicry can take striking forms, as in the case of the butterfly with mimic eyes upon its wings to divert an attacking bird's attention from more vital parts. Some moths and butterflies show beak marks on and around these mimic-eye targets. These insects were saved in action by clever camouflage; camouflage to divert, not to conceal.

It is simpler to fool wildlife than it is to fool an enemy camera, so the camoufleur should be warned to use nature's tricks with caution. A modern attacker *looks* for camouflage.

# THEORY OF RECOGNITION
## 5

Practical camouflage calls for the elimination or reduction of the qualities by which we recognize an object.

The factors in visual recognition are four: We recognize an object by its *color, texture, shape* and *shadow*. Our camouflage technique must be applied to each of these factors. For instance, we would observe that the haystack in the field (Fig. 9) is yellowish, rough, round, and resting on the ground. If we want to camouflage this haystack, we should ask ourselves:—

1) Does the haystack's color match surrounding colors?
2) Does its texture match surrounding textures?
3) Can we disrupt its shape?
4) Can we disguise its revealing shadow?

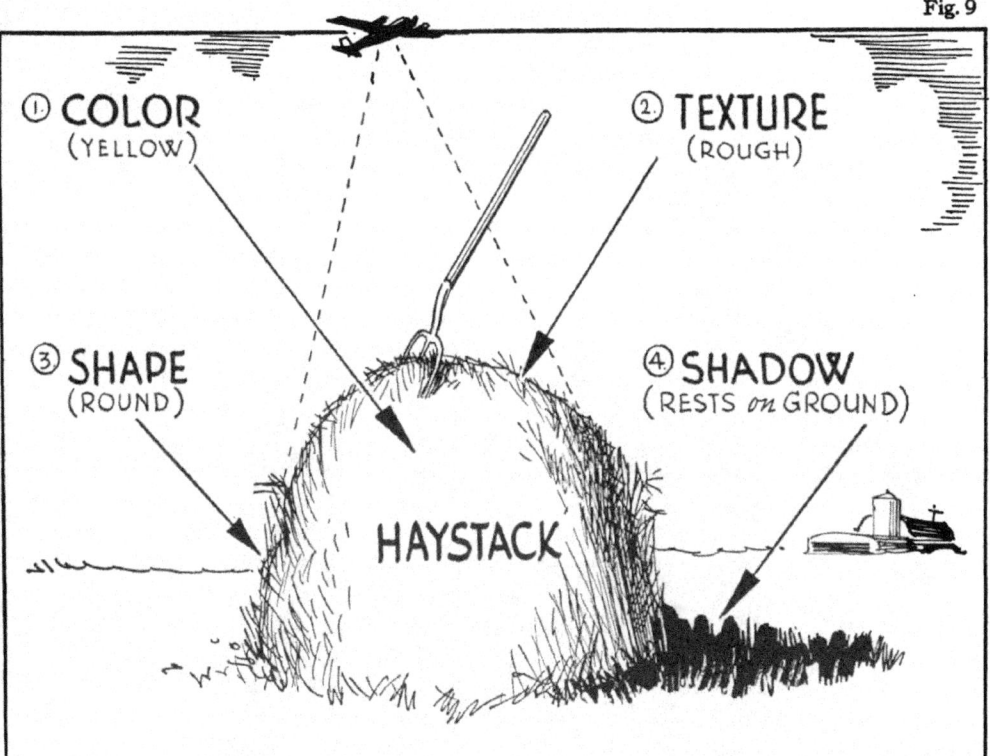

Fig. 9

① COLOR (YELLOW)  ② TEXTURE (ROUGH)

③ SHAPE (ROUND)  ④ SHADOW (RESTS *on* GROUND)

HAYSTACK

With the *reduction of the differences* in color, texture, shape and shadow between it and its background, we can make the haystack approach invisibility.

(Fig. 10) shows the actual application of this theory. It is accomplished by three basic methods: By concealment; by disruption; by mimicry. This simplified chart may help the student of camouflage to classify and memorize the methods that will be described in the following pages. Military adaptations of these methods are wide and varied but the trend is always toward sound concealment and away from trick designs that can be picked up by the infra-red ray camera. Also it must be remembered in each camouflage installation, the vital importance of keeping all signs of human activity out of sight, such as wheel and foot tracks, smoke, automobiles, and lights.

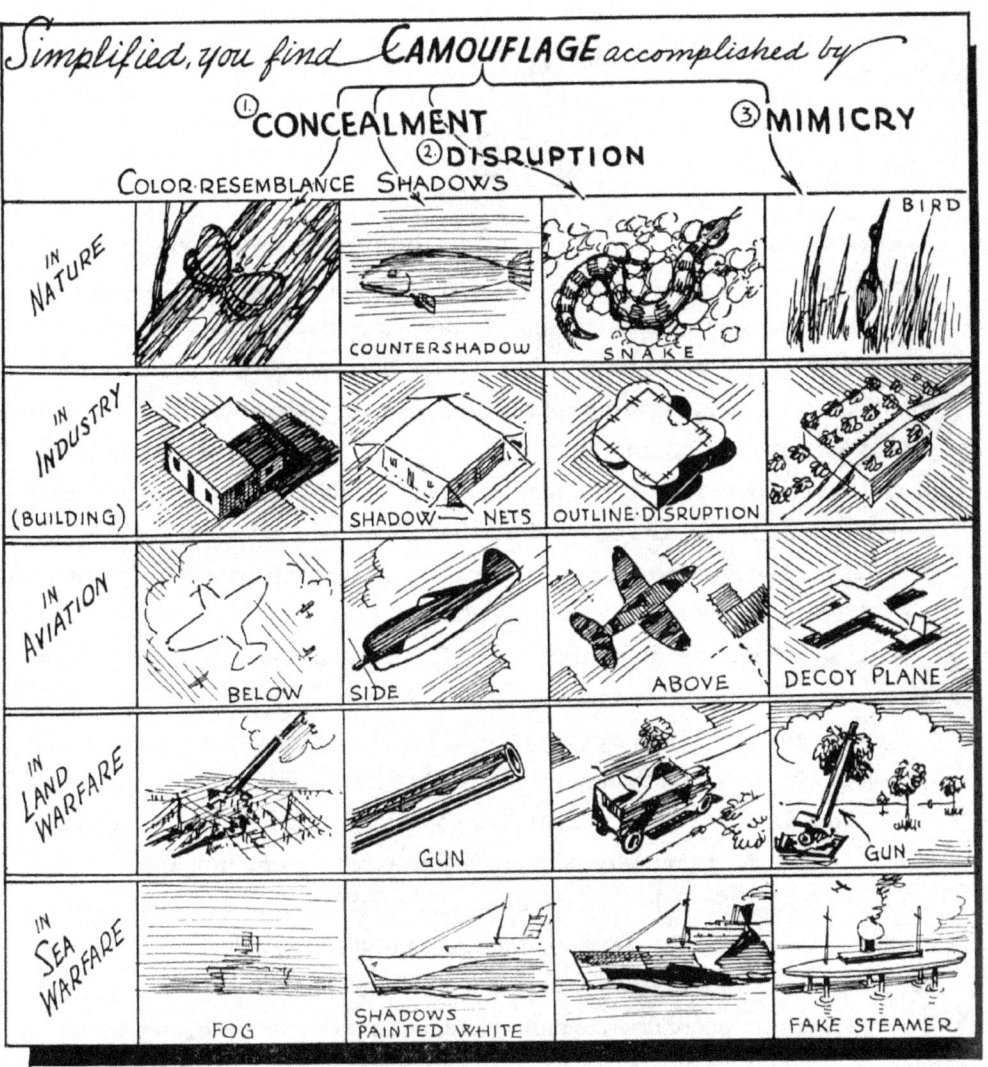

Fig. 10

# COLOR RESEMBLANCE

## 6

Examples (A) and (B) (Fig. 11) showing the effect of a small white sheet of paper lying upon a larger white sheet, and a small black sheet upon a larger black sheet, demonstrate the theory of color resemblance in concealment. Of course the speeding plane cannot always resemble the ground beneath in exact color, but if we take an average of green foliage, dark water and brown fields we have a general shade of muddy green as a happy medium, which most planes have adopted for their upper coloring. For their bellies, a flat white is generally used so that the observer on the ground will not see a dark shape, or the shaded under portion of the ship. For night attack, planes are painted a dull black so as not to reflect searchlight rays.

As seen from the air, a green lawn (C) may become a landmark, and a white concrete runway or parking area (D) may become a perfect target; such areas are easily colored to correspond with the surrounding land (E).

It is with color resemblance however that the novice is apt to overdo his camouflage. Distance tends to *bring out* color rather than to dull it. Holding an oil painting close, you see a blur of indefinite color but holding it afar, each color stands out. So it is safer to under-color rather than over-color when painting camouflage. Choose dull, dark green and slate patterns. Remember you are painting out a target, not making a target (F).

Coloring is not confined to paint work, but may need living grass, shrubs, cinders, Spanish moss, sawdust or any suitable and convenient material. When actual paint is required the list of paints prepared by the War Department may be referred to.

Battleships cannot be treated perfectly for color resemblance because their backgrounds are constantly changing. From the water's surface this background is often a bright horizon that silhouettes their shape. However a dull blue-grey shade blends with most fog and night conditions, and at such

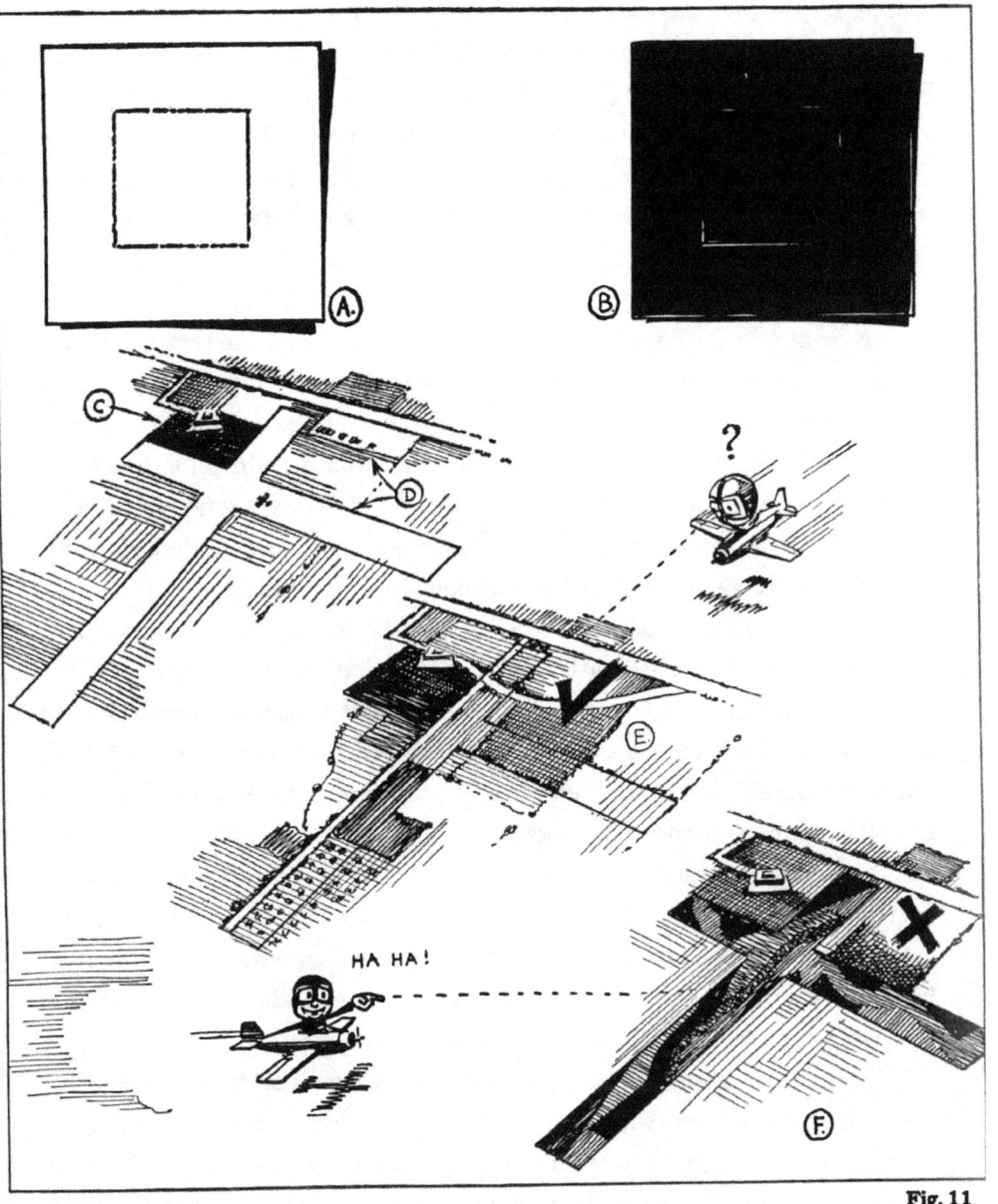

Fig. 11

times a ship enjoys comparative safety because of its camouflage.

On land too, similar problems occur, for seasons cause an ever-changing background and camouflage coloration must change with them. Of course snow will cover everything and is often a boon to camouflage.

Under certain conditions, a building (A) (Fig. 12) could be made to resemble tilled land (B) and the land surrounding it be kept tilled; or actual vegetation could even be grown upon a roof and counted upon to change with the natural surrounding vegetation.

Nets or wires woven with cloth strips are used to good effect, but where bright green cloth is used, the color may be expected to fade to a gray tone before long and a new spray of paint will then have to be applied. Where nets hold actual tree branches, the leaves soon curl and turn in color, becoming conspicuous and in need of replacement. Even metal-grass (scrap-metal wool matting with the texture of grass) needs servicing and preparation, for rusty metal turns orange-red, a most conspicuous color from the air.

Where large areas of concrete, or light colored roads, runways and loading areas are to be blended with a paint application, the whole area may first be toned to a dark shade with a spray of asphalt or tar emulsion. Diluted wood stains are also of value, especially where foliage is to be added. But these flat surfaces will wear away under heavy traffic and accentuate the presence of trucks, airplanes and other mobile equipment. They will need frequent servicing. Where traffic is heavy as in airplane runways or road crossings, protective coloring may be applied to coarse sawdust, chopped rubber, or crushed stone, which are spread upon the asphalt or tar emulsion. This covering will wear better and the color will remain longer under traffic. Nevertheless, frequent sweepings and new applications are necessary.

Color resemblance accomplished by paint alone is often impossible. For instance, if grass were painted on a canvas strip and placed on a real grass plot, the effect might deceive an observer from a few feet away. Yet on an aerial photograph taken a mile and a half in the air, the painting which would do nothing but reflect light from its smooth surface would appear white while

28

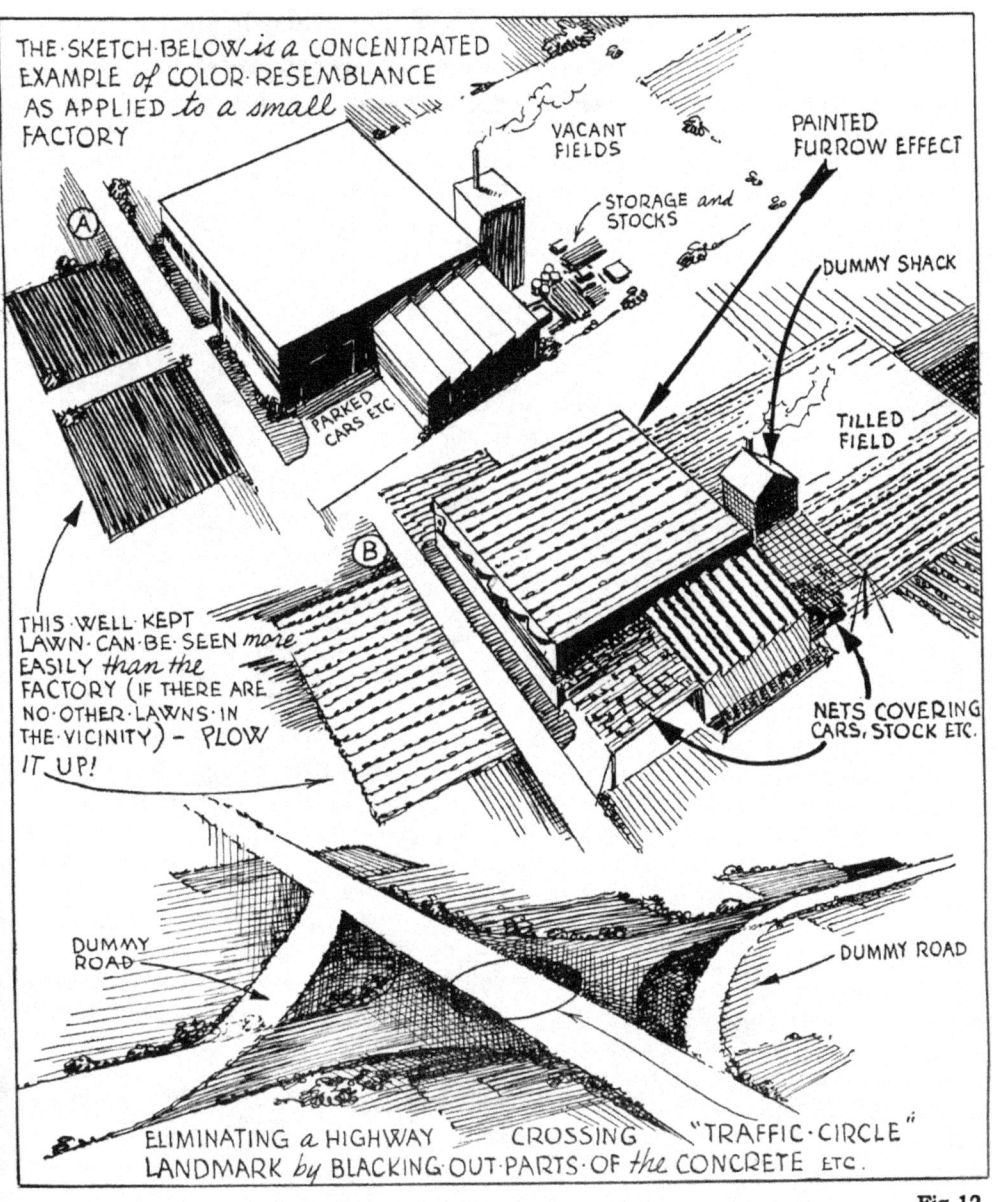

THE·SKETCH·BELOW *is a* CONCENTRATED EXAMPLE *of* COLOR·RESEMBLANCE AS APPLIED *to a small* FACTORY

Ⓐ

VACANT FIELDS

STORAGE *and* STOCKS

PAINTED FURROW EFFECT

DUMMY SHACK

PARKED CARS ETC

TILLED FIELD

Ⓑ

THIS·WELL·KEPT LAWN·CAN·BE·SEEN *more* EASILY *than the* FACTORY (IF THERE ARE NO·OTHER·LAWNS·IN THE·VICINITY) – PLOW IT UP!

NETS COVERING CARS, STOCK ETC.

DUMMY ROAD

DUMMY ROAD

ELIMINATING *a* HIGHWAY CROSSING "TRAFFIC·CIRCLE" LANDMARK *by* BLACKING·OUT·PARTS·OF *the* CONCRETE ETC.

Fig. 12

the real grass would register in light grey. This is because the painting lacks proper texture. Color therefore is of much less importance in modern camouflage than it formerly was because, as already stressed, aerial photography has become the chief means of detecting concealed objects.

# THE SHADOW PROBLEM

# 7

The shadow problem is one of the greatest problems in camouflage. (A) (Fig. 13) shows a chimney from overhead; the actual chimney can hardly be seen but the shadow (B) is not only pronounced but magnified. This shadow can not be painted out because it moves with the sun, making the larger smokestacks and towers quite unconcealable. (C) shows a method of wiring a smokestack, draping it with nets and woven material to cast a diffused and disrupted shadow; this solution is good under certain conditions, but wind and weather, and the size of the stack itself offer handicaps. The best solution would be to eliminate the chimney and substitute a forced draft system. Notice that a shadow can indicate the height of its subject although from overhead the view without the shadow would be deceiving.

As a rough rule of thumb it may be stated that an object will cast shadows from three to six feet long for every foot of its height, according to the time of day, month of the year and latitude. This becomes important to the aerial photographer studying developed prints. By using the rule he can often translate a shadow into that cast by a known but otherwise concealed target.

Fig. 13

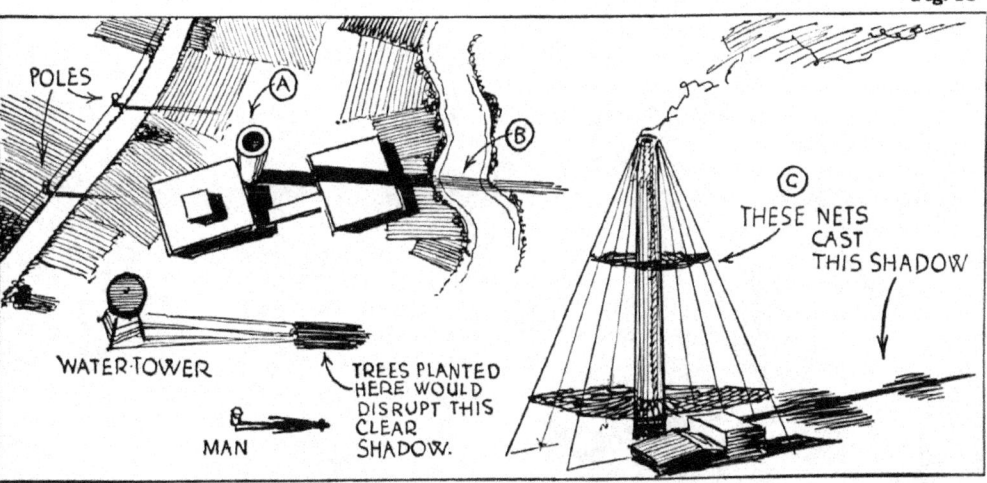

A row of gables or saw-tooth partitions making up a roof, might be set at such an angle to the sun as not to show its angular surfaces, but the shadow that this roof throws would be a telltale patch (D Fig. 14).

Fig. 14 gives some examples of shadow catching devices. The less the angle of nets or partitions, the more effective they will be. Every case of shadow offers a different problem with different heights, shapes and attitudes toward the sun. The problem can only be met by a designer with an adaptive, creative mind.

As noted, an object is often less conspicuous than its shadow. When disrupting a field or flat surface, it is better not to paint in shadows, but to create actual shadows that move naturally with the sun.

Hedges can be painted on large flat surfaces by applying lamp black in an irregular shadow patch on the grass or earth; but such a shadow will not move with the sunlight, therefore when disruptive shadows are needed to break up flat surfaces or sharp building shadows, artificial trees offer the simpler solution.

In designing shadow catching nets, especially when automobiles are to be run under them, stress must be laid on good engineering. Winds, rain and heavy snow will cause weak nets to sag and break. In winding cloth strips through nets, a good portion of the cloth should be left unwound to hang freely, causing a swaying, moving shadow. The man constructing a tree frame in (Fig. 15) is getting this effect.

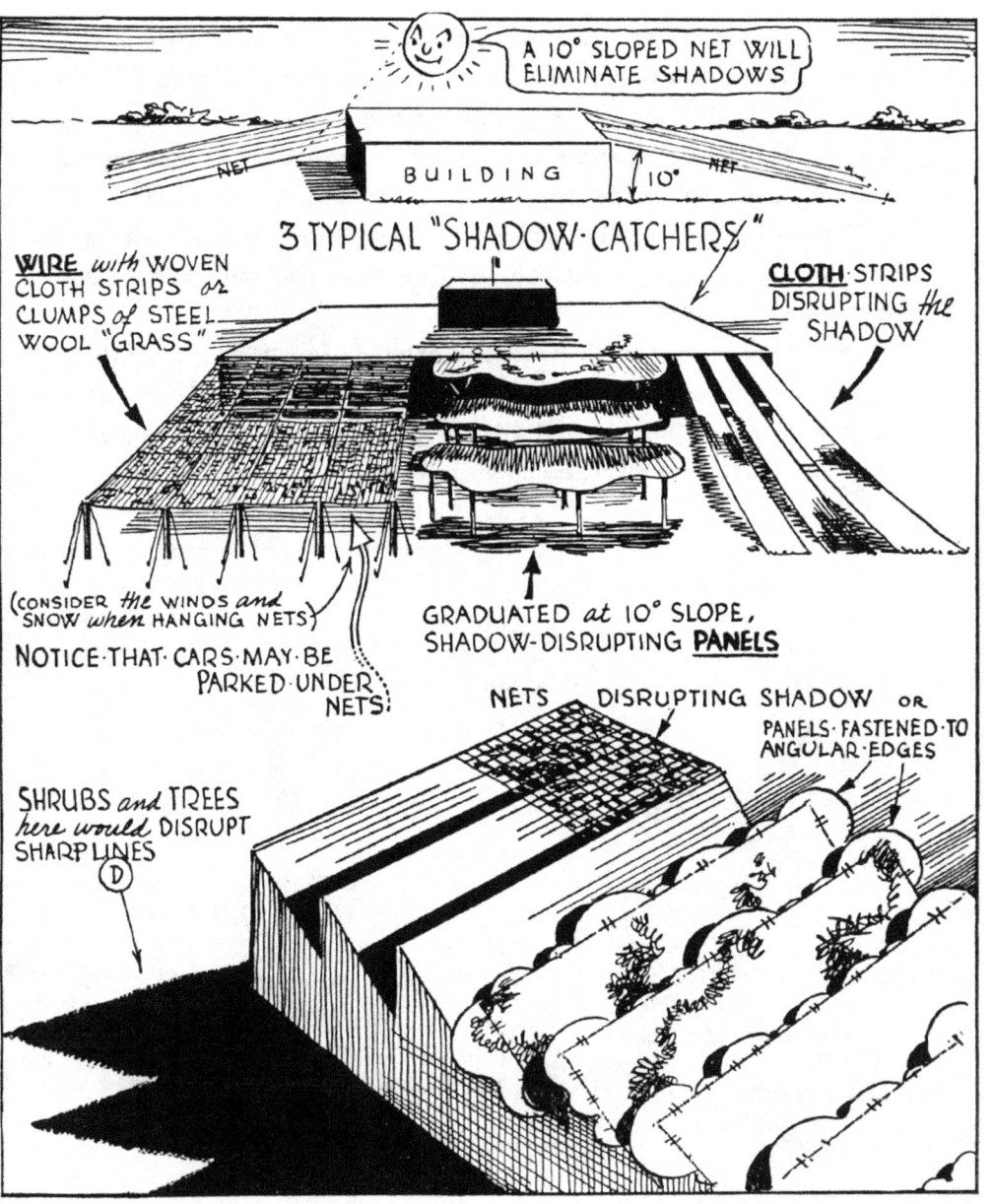

A 10° SLOPED NET WILL ELIMINATE SHADOWS

BUILDING    10°

NET    NET

## 3 TYPICAL "SHADOW·CATCHERS"

**WIRE** *with* WOVEN CLOTH STRIPS *or* CLUMPS *of* STEEL WOOL "GRASS"

**CLOTH**·STRIPS DISRUPTING *the* SHADOW

(CONSIDER *the* WINDS *and* SNOW *when* HANGING NETS)

NOTICE·THAT·CARS·MAY·BE PARKED·UNDER NETS

GRADUATED *at* 10° SLOPE, SHADOW·DISRUPTING **PANELS**

SHRUBS *and* TREES *here would* DISRUPT SHARP·LINES
Ⓓ

NETS    DISRUPTING SHADOW OR PANELS·FASTENED·TO ANGULAR·EDGES

Fig. 14

(Fig. 15) shows artificial trees and shapes designed to create a disruptive pattern of shadow which can hide men, equipment or a flat surface. In the case of an airfield or open loading area, movable "trees" on wheels can be placed in the open during an air raid. The tree made of old tin cans (painted green) demonstrates how refuse can be put to good use for concealment. Old rags if draped and arranged irregularly, will cast disrupting shadows on and around airplanes, guns and valuable equipment and help disguise their telltale outlines.

Real trees planted in the shaded area of buildings will disrupt that shade provided they are tall enough for their tops to reach over the shadow. Real trees or shrubs are to be preferred when practicable for as we have noted the aerial camera can show up artificial foliage.

Fig. 15

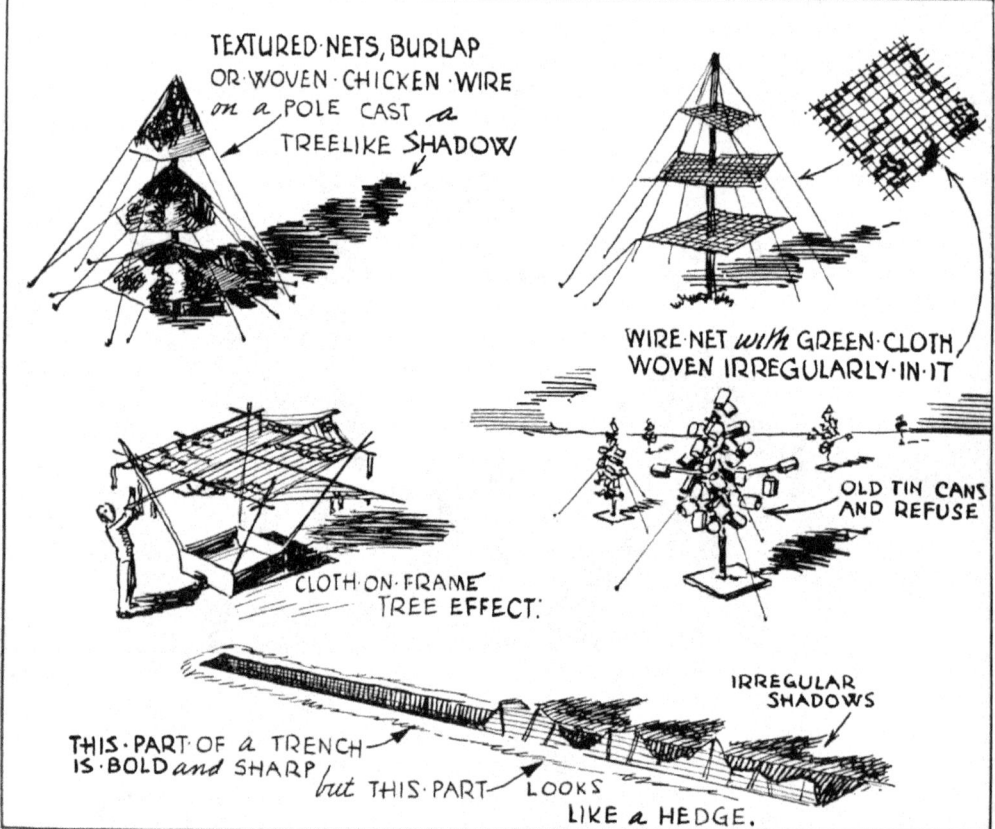

# DISRUPTION IN CAMOUFLAGE

## 8

Disruption in camouflage can be accomplished by distorting the outline, the shadow, the surface texture, or even the distance of the subject. Distance can be disrupted by the dazzle design which will often cause an attacker to over-shoot or under-shoot a target; and this same dazzle can also disrupt the shape of the target and spoil the attacker's aim. Nature often uses this pattern as shown in (Fig. 17), and this was the first camouflage pattern painted on World War I troopships. These dazzles did not necessarily conceal; in fact too often they called attention to the subject; but the theory held that if an attacker had sighted the ship, the best that could be done would be to spoil his aim. Modern camouflage calls more for principles of sound concealment than for this obvious splashy treatment.

(Fig. 17) shows an airplane painted with a dazzle design, and yet however effective this pattern may be for a special terrain, the amount of paint needed to accomplish the design is a serious detriment. To begin with, dull paint application to airplanes is a handicap because such a surface creates more friction. Furthermore, paint has weight and therefore would seriously reduce speed. One lightly sprayed on coat adds 37 pounds to the average small bomber.

All in all, (Figs. 16 & 17) show a side of camouflage most dangerous to attempt. The disruptive applications on the following pages are sounder and can also be applied to industrial concealment.

Fig. 16

THE·BUTTERFLY *uses* a DISRUPTIVE·DESIGN *to take your eye from* VITAL PARTS __ MIMIC·"EYES" *or* BULLS·EYES *are "painted" on* WING·SECTIONS *merely to* CAUSE BIRDS *to* BITE *there instead of* VITAL BODY REGIONS.

THIS "ATTENTION GETTER" IS KNOWN *as* "ALLURING *and* MIMETIC·RESEMBLANCE" *in* NATURE'S PROTECTIVE·BAG OF·TRICKS. IN MODERN WARFARE, *when an enemy is sighted and the range* IS CLOSE, *we may use this* "ALLURING RESEMBLANCE" DESIGN *to make him* MISS·HIS·MARK *or as in the case of the* SHIP BELOW, ATTENTION *is directed to* BOW *and* STERN *and* AWAY *from* SHIP'S CENTER

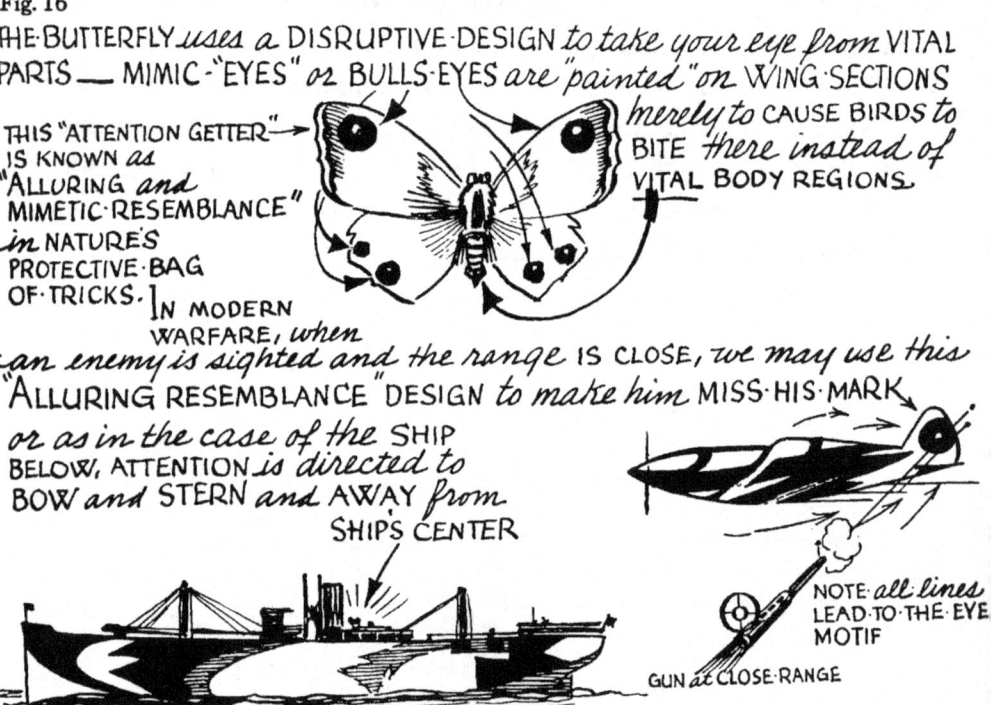

NOTE: *all lines* LEAD·TO·THE·EYE MOTIF

GUN *at* CLOSE·RANGE

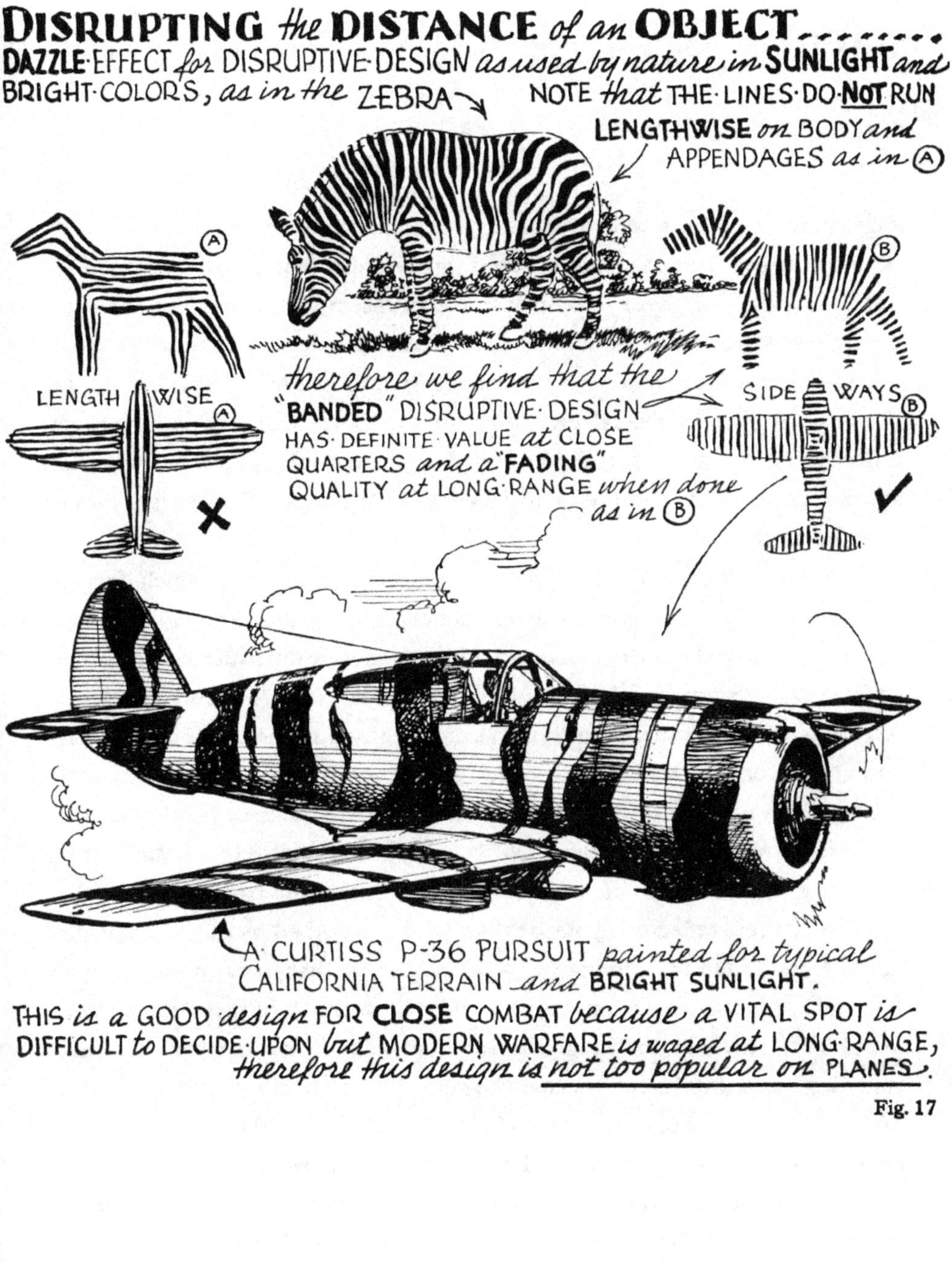

# DISRUPTING the DISTANCE of an OBJECT.........

DAZZLE·EFFECT for DISRUPTIVE·DESIGN as used by nature in SUNLIGHT and BRIGHT·COLORS, as in the ZEBRA ➘

NOTE that THE·LINES·DO·NOT RUN LENGTHWISE on BODY and APPENDAGES as in Ⓐ

LENGTH WISE Ⓐ

✕

therefore we find that the "BANDED" DISRUPTIVE·DESIGN HAS·DEFINITE·VALUE at CLOSE QUARTERS and a "FADING" QUALITY at LONG·RANGE when done as in Ⓑ

SIDE WAYS Ⓑ

✔

A·CURTISS P-36 PURSUIT painted for typical CALIFORNIA TERRAIN and BRIGHT SUNLIGHT.

THIS is a GOOD design FOR CLOSE COMBAT because a VITAL SPOT is DIFFICULT to DECIDE·UPON but MODERN WARFARE is waged at LONG·RANGE, therefore this design is not too popular on PLANES.

Fig. 17

# DISRUPTION OF SURFACE TEXTURE

## 9

An airplane runway, a concrete road and a factory roof stand out prominently because their surface texture differs sharply from that of the surrounding terrain. Disrupting these smooth surfaces to resemble the surrounding area becomes the task of the camoufleur. A flat concrete runway cannot make use of raised shadow makers without destroying its function. But in hiding the flatness, irregular "surfaces" can be painted in. Since ordinary paint is more reflective than natural surroundings it will photograph lighter, hence either solids must be added to the paint to roughen it or special lusterless paints must be used.

In the drawing (A) (Fig. 18) we see a typical fake gully, which is made by painting a dark patch after the manner of a stream bed, with light patches scattered about where the banks would be. A more subtle disruption can be effected by carrying the design right off the flat surface (B) and to the surrounding area, using lampblack or dye on the grass. In the case of an airport, actual trees or fake trees can be quickly distributed about the vital area, by rolling them out to designated spots during air raid alarms. And wherever practical, a furrowed or plowed field is easily simulated as in (C) and (D).

The shadow value of textures plays an important part in surface disruption. Light is reflected by flat surfaces but is absorbed by dull uneven surfaces. A good plan for eliminating window glare is first to paint on a coat of flat black, then to smear on a spatter coat of dark green paint mixed with about 25% sawdust. Painting grass on a flat smooth roof to blend with surrounding grass would not conceal the roof, for at certain angles, no matter how rough the grass pattern was made to seem, there would be a flat reflection causing the disguise to disappear. Therefore, a texture similar to the surrounding grass would have to be introduced. Wood shavings, excelsior, brushwood, sawdust, moss, or discarded shreds from industrial plants can be applied

**38**

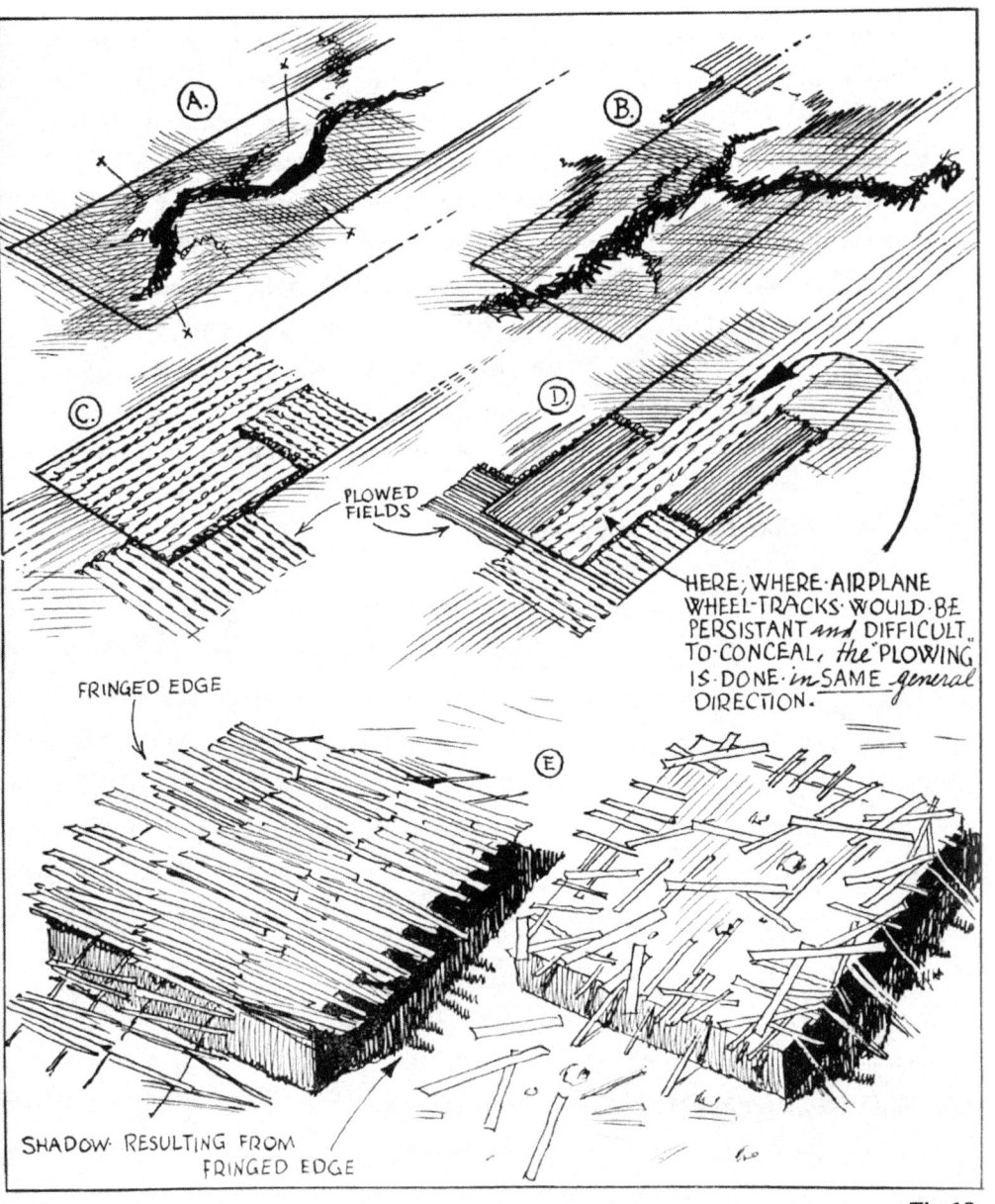

A.

B.

C.

D.

PLOWED
FIELDS

HERE; WHERE · AIRPLANE
WHEEL·TRACKS· WOULD· BE
PERSISTANT *and* DIFFICULT,
TO· CONCEAL, *the* "PLOWING"
IS · DONE · *in* SAME *general*
DIRECTION ·

FRINGED EDGE

E

SHADOW· RESULTING FROM
FRINGED EDGE

Fig. 18

directly to a tar or glue base and dyed with paint or creosote stains. A neater if more temporary job can be done by applying the texture to chicken wire and stretching it out wherever needed. Other texturing materials are: cinders, pineapple tops, corncob chips, pine cones, glass or steel wool, silage and sand. The camouflage section of the Engineer Board has compiled a technical manual, *Materials for Protective Concealment* (TM 5-269, Supt. of Documents, Washington, D. C.) which will be of great help to the student.

Texture is a telltale of human activity. One man walking over a wet lawn leaves a trail that can be seen from the air as distinctly as that trail a snake would make as it proceeds through a sanded road. One may imagine then how tire tracks would show up on grass or rough dirt. In making a dummy factory or airfield, heavy vehicles would have to be run many times over the area to simulate the customary tracks.

40

# DISRUPTION OF OUTLINE
## 10

Other than a bright sun reflection shining in a bombardier's eyes from a factory's windows, the most important attention getter is a distinct outline. It is usually this outline he is looking for. In sunlight, the shadow matching this outline only helps to make it more conspicuous. The business of disrupting this outline is then of great importance. Of course creating a new but very conspicuous outline is just as bad as no disruption.

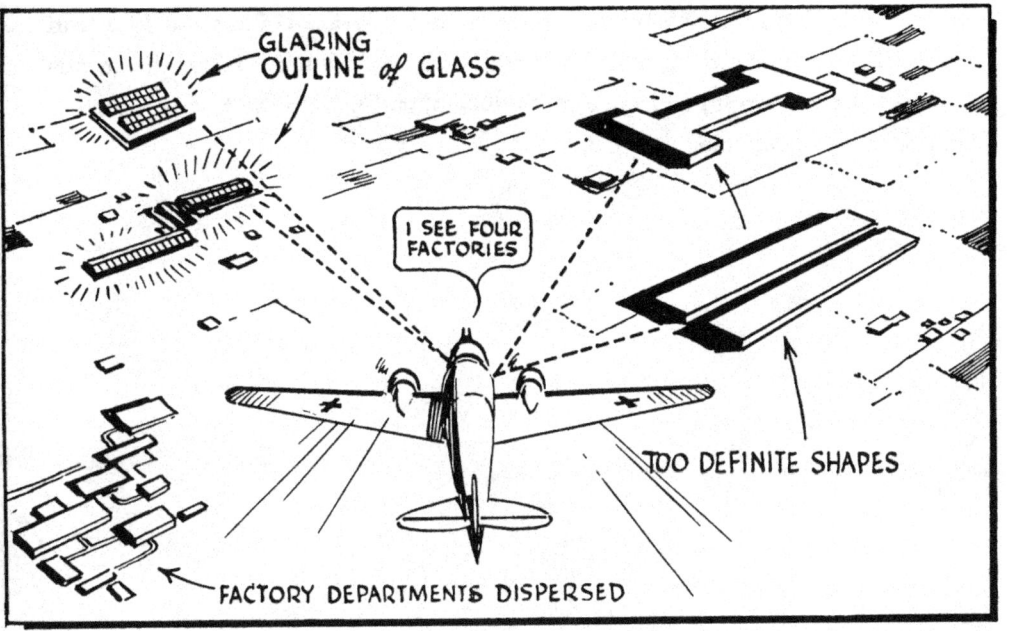

Fig. 18a

Factories usually have very definite shape and are so concentrated that concealment is difficult. A perfectly designed industrial building is usually an imperfectly designed defense factory, for manufacturers generally strive to keep the production line and accessory departments under one roof. The wartime factory should be divided into many small structures, irregularly arranged for camouflaging and at proper distances for protection against bombing. In (Fig. 19), notice (A) and then look at the same shape with flaps on the roof to distort the outline (B). In the case of a row of similar buildings or of turrets on a single roof, each can be treated in this manner and about half of them irregularly connected as in (C).

Any lengthy straight line in a building and any round or squarish outline should be broken up. Pick out these features in the drawing. (D).

Remember that in applying new outlines to a building, it is simple to construct a cardboard model with great flaps hanging out unsupported, but in actual construction there are winds, snow and structural handicaps to contend with. Too solid a shield will collapse under pressure of snow and ice, and although composition boards and solid wood panels are effective from airplane heights, a semi-solid net, cloth woven, will usually be just as effective and far more durable.

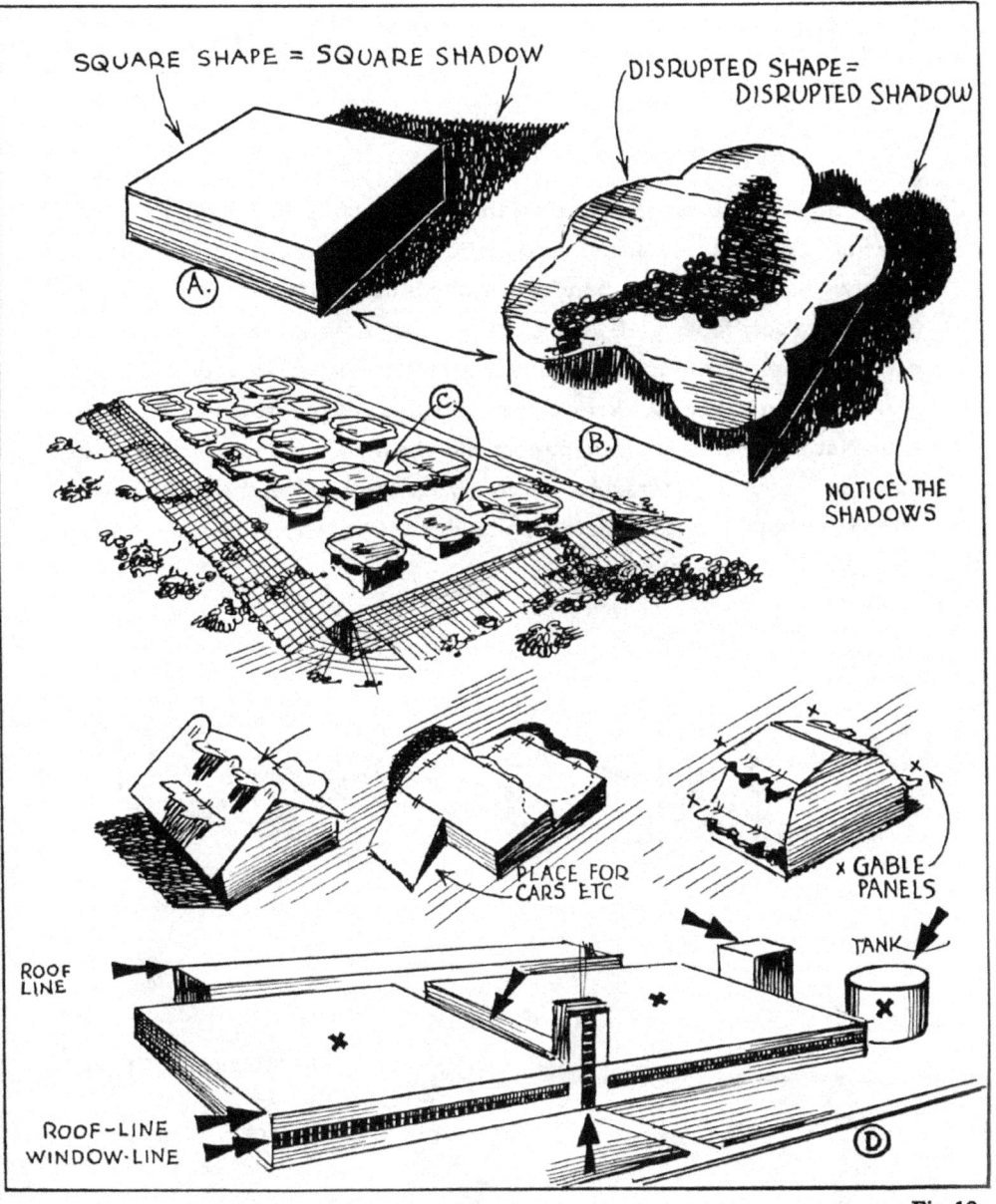

Fig. 19

# DISRUPTION AS AN ART

## II

To an attacking bomber searching the pattern of ground landscape for a camouflaged objective, elaborate coloration and radical disruptive design are give-aways. Any square or round shape stands out in sharp contrast to rolling terrain and soft foliage. (See A. Fig. 20). Any unusual shape in a painted pattern such as (B) (Fig. 21) acts as an attention getter; from one badly done part of a pattern, the attacker can spot and pick out the rest of a camouflage plan. Nature weaves fantastic designs but she avoids round or angular patterns, or monotonously regular curves. Irregularity is what the camoufleur should seek at all times when designing disruptive concealment. Regularity invariably indicates human activity.

Fig. 20

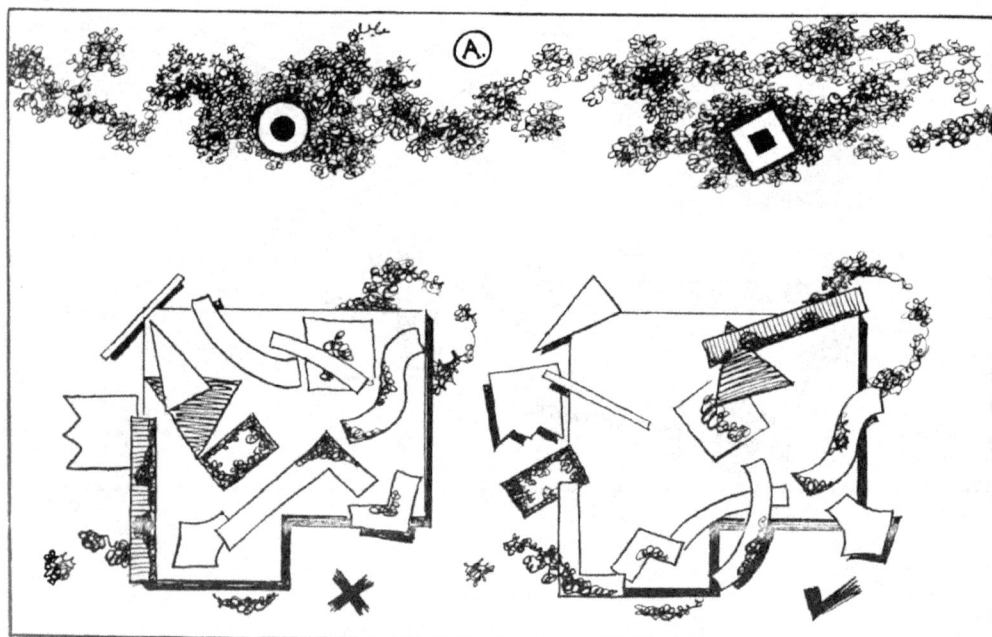

Notice in (Fig. 20) how a set of identical shapes can be placed first badly and then successfully to disrupt a certain outline. In this case a model is valuable for it is simpler to experiment with disruptive pattern on cardboard than on actual roof or field.

REGARDING·IRREGULAR·PATTERNS

Fig. 21

Ⓑ

THIS·SHAPE STANDS·OUT LIKE *a* SORE THUMB

HERE *is a* TYPICAL·DISRUPTIVE·PATTERN **But** IT HAS *a* TOO·DEFINED·SHAPE *that acts as an* ATTENTION·GETTER. *This* SHAPE *needs a* "BLENDING·OUT".... BY SQUINTING·THE·EYE, *an* ATTENTION·GETTER *can be readily* DETECTED *and* CORRECTED.

*Of* COURSE, "ATTENTION·GETTERS" *may take the* AIM *of a* GUNNER· *away* FROM VITAL PARTS *but this is more* FOR BUTTERFLIES— NOT 300 M.P.H. PLANES.

ANOTHER·ATTENTION-GETTER *is too* REGULAR *a* PATTERN DONE EITHER *with* MECHANICAL·REGULARITY— — —*or*— — —RHYTHMIC·REGULARITY (CURVES ALL ALIKE)

X { TOO·REGULAR A·PATTERN

*Nature avoids regular repetition*

(ROOF ON BUILDING)

MORAL: *While* DISRUPTING *the* CONTOUR, DON'T PAINT *in a* BULL'S·EYE X

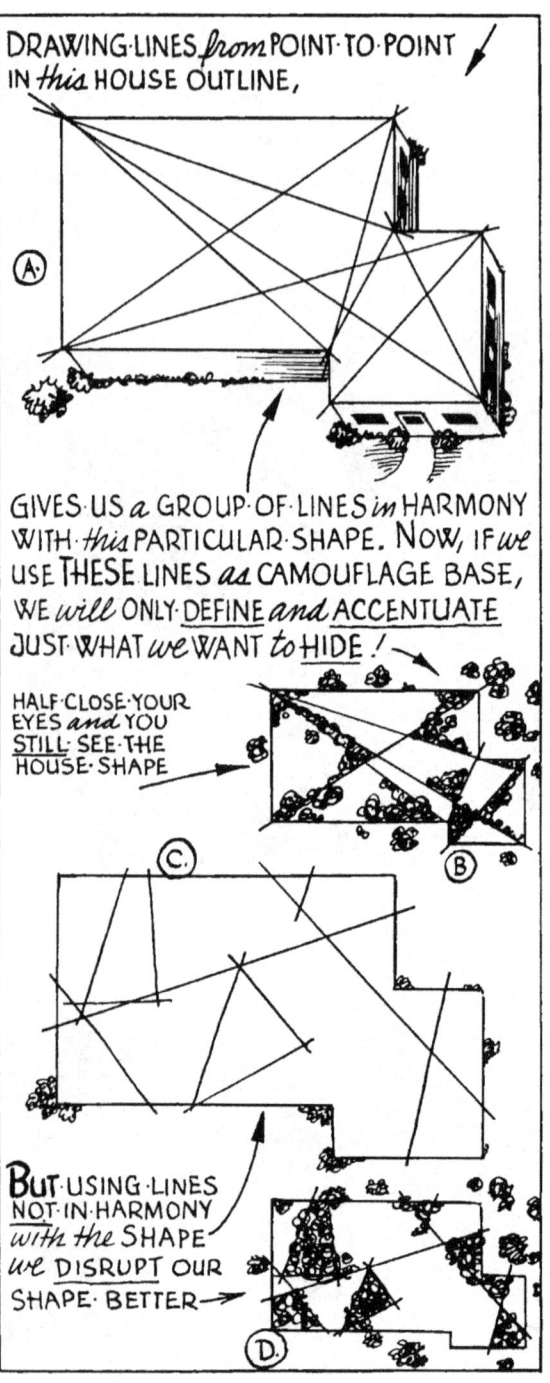

DRAWING·LINES *from* POINT·TO·POINT IN *this* HOUSE OUTLINE,

(A)

GIVES·US *a* GROUP·OF·LINES *in* HARMONY WITH·*this* PARTICULAR·SHAPE. NOW, IF *we* USE THESE LINES *as* CAMOUFLAGE·BASE, WE *will* ONLY·DEFINE *and* ACCENTUATE JUST·WHAT *we* WANT *to* HIDE !

HALF·CLOSE·YOUR EYES *and* YOU STILL·SEE·THE HOUSE·SHAPE

(C)

(B)

BUT·USING·LINES NOT·IN·HARMONY *with the* SHAPE *we* DISRUPT OUR SHAPE· BETTER→

(D)

# THE DISRUPTIVE PATTERN

## 12

A formula is often used by artists and advertising men to get dynamic layout composition. The practice is to make straight lines from the corners of the shape of the layout, and more lines from any intersection or point thereon. Logically then, these lines will all be in harmony with the shape they are in. A composition drawn over it will also harmonize. In (Fig. 22) a factory shape (A) has been treated with similar lines, from point to point. As these lines are in harmony with the shape they will tend to accentuate it; therefore such lines must be avoided in disruptive camouflage (B).

By using lines that do not harmonize with the shape, we get a disrupted mass (C). Using these lines for a base over which to place our disruptive pattern we get a good disruptive camouflage design (D).

Fig. 22

This technique can be used in disrupting any shape. In (Fig. 23) we see an airplane, a difficult shape to disrupt because it is so dynamic. In (A1) the plane has been mapped out with harmonious lines, and in (A2) these lines have been followed through with a camouflage effort that is slightly confusing but still accentuates the shape of the airplane. In (A3) we see a dazzle design in which all patterns are out of shape. The result is complete disharmony and good disruption of outline. This theory can be used for the placement or parking of automobiles, and anywhere that disruption is of use in concealing a shape.

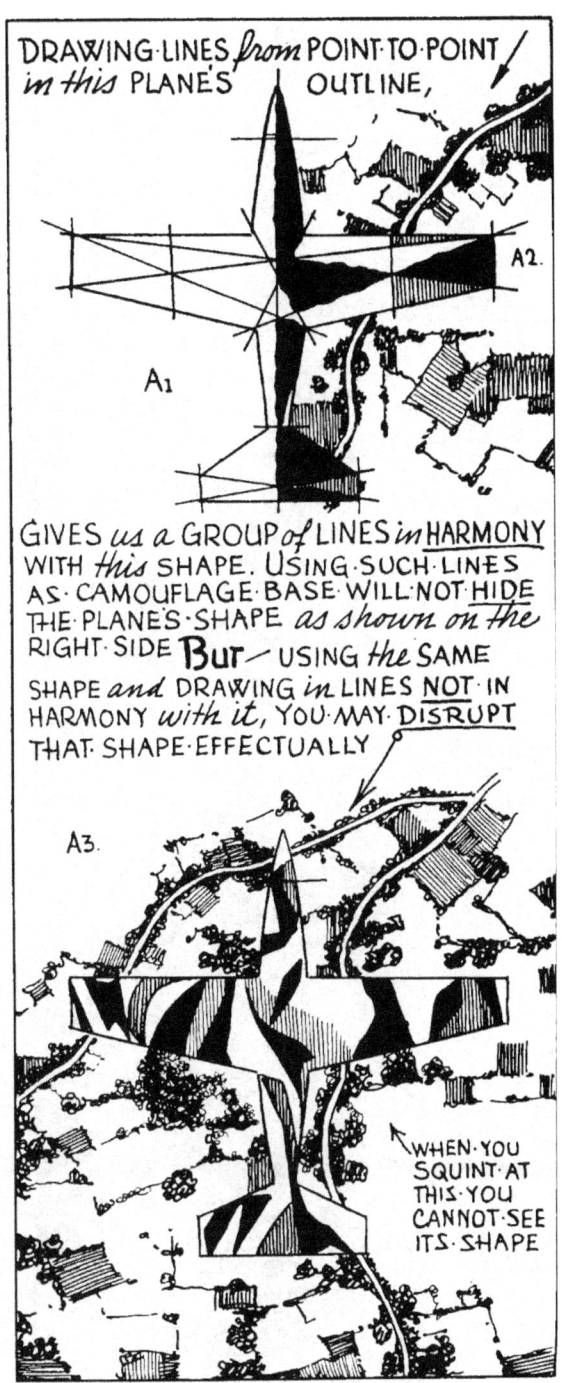

DRAWING·LINES *from* POINT·TO·POINT *in this* PLANE'S OUTLINE,

A2.

A1

GIVES *us a* GROUP *of* LINES *in* HARMONY WITH *this* SHAPE. USING·SUCH·LINES AS·CAMOUFLAGE·BASE·WILL·NOT·HIDE THE·PLANE'S·SHAPE *as shown on the* RIGHT·SIDE But— USING *the* SAME SHAPE *and* DRAWING *in* LINES NOT·IN HARMONY *with it,* YOU·MAY·DISRUPT THAT·SHAPE·EFFECTUALLY

A3.

WHEN·YOU SQUINT·AT THIS·YOU CANNOT·SEE ITS·SHAPE

Fig. 23

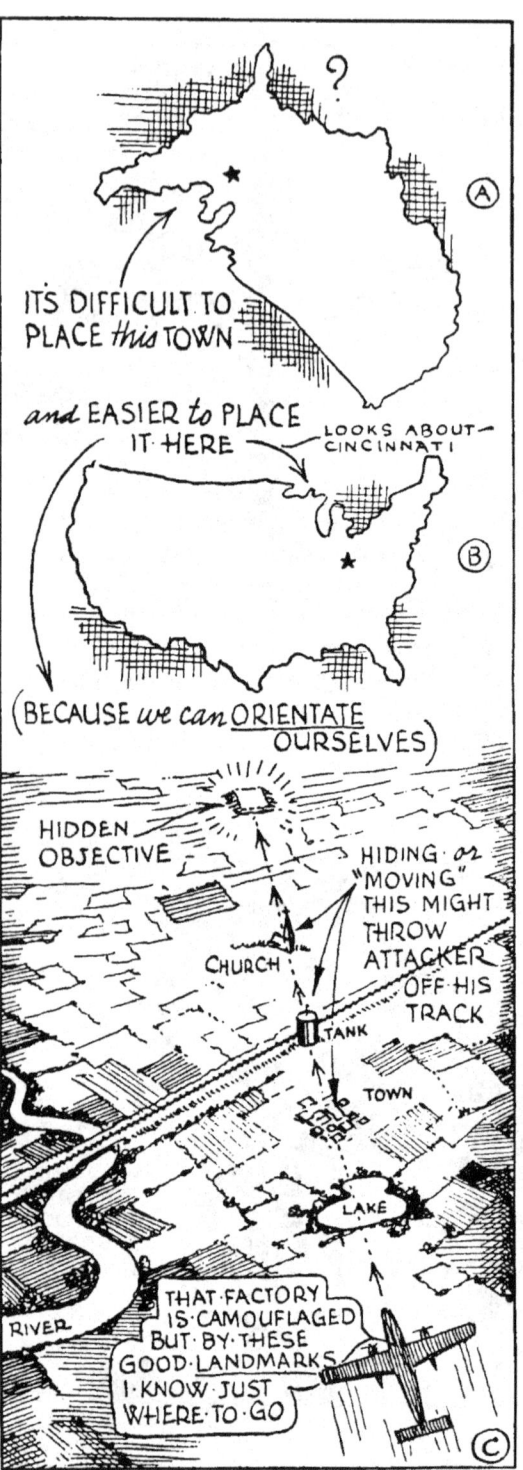

Fig. 24

# DISRUPTION OF LANDMARKS

## 13

The pilot proceeds toward his objective constantly checking on landmarks such as railroads, tanks, lakes and factories. When references are hidden or moved, the job of bombing becomes more difficult. Hiding or moving landmarks is definitely a part of any major camouflage job. Of course, most landmarks are immovable and un-concealable, so this theory of disruption by disorientation works best during the night when real towns can be blacked out and dummy towns and factories set out to disorientate the attacker. If you don't think disruption can be effected by moving landmarks, look at (A) (Fig. 24) and see if you can at once locate the star. Now look at (B)—See how easy it is to locate because you are accustomed to seeing the U. S. in this attitude.

# THE USE OF MIMICRY

## 14

As most attacks have a definite objective, and the concealment of that objective will lead the enemy to search for it in a camouflaged state, mimicry is used in landmarks. (Fig. 25) shows a small factory conspicuous because of landmarks:—The church, the main road, and the branch road. In (2) the factory has been moved in dummy form to the right, while the church and road are hidden. The real factory has had a dummy steeple placed over its stack and the real church's steeple has been temporarily removed. The whole effect is confusing to a pilot who orientates himself by a map and landmark details.

A false factory must not be too conspicuous and should even be camouflaged a bit. False windows and lights, smoke pots and other smoke effects will help to make the dummy look real. The camoufleur with imagination is at his best in the field of mimicry.

Fig. 25

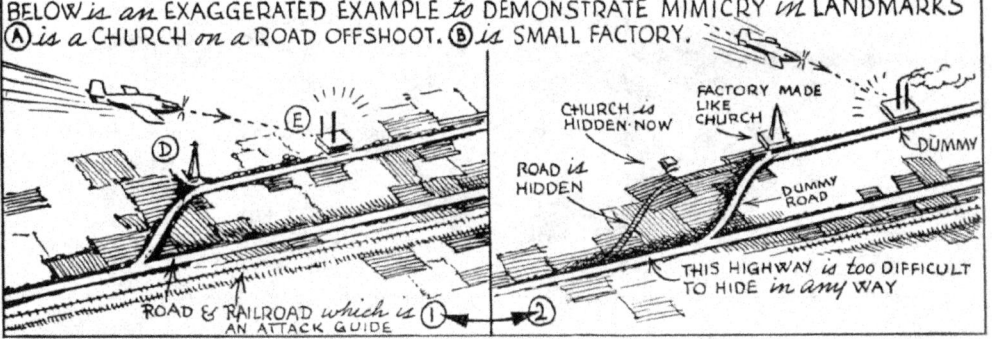

BELOW _is an_ EXAGGERATED EXAMPLE _to_ DEMONSTRATE MIMICRY _in_ LANDMARKS
Ⓐ _is a_ CHURCH _on a_ ROAD OFFSHOOT. Ⓑ _is_ SMALL FACTORY.

CHURCH _is_ HIDDEN·NOW

FACTORY MADE LIKE CHURCH

ROAD _is_ HIDDEN

DUMMY

DUMMY ROAD

THIS HIGHWAY _is too_ DIFFICULT TO HIDE _in any_ WAY

ROAD & RAILROAD _which is_ ① AN ATTACK GUIDE

②

Artificial airplanes made from canvas and poles are effective when stacked out at the end of a trail of mimic wheel tracks in the ground. In heavily bombed towns, whole sections have been mimicked, with barges filling river basins to represent tenement house blocks, and heavy canvas strips draped over lofty buildings to simulate streets and highways. (Fig. 26) shows a mimic village community on a rooftop and a panel and canvas strip "roadway" successfully breaking up a factory outline.

Fig. 26

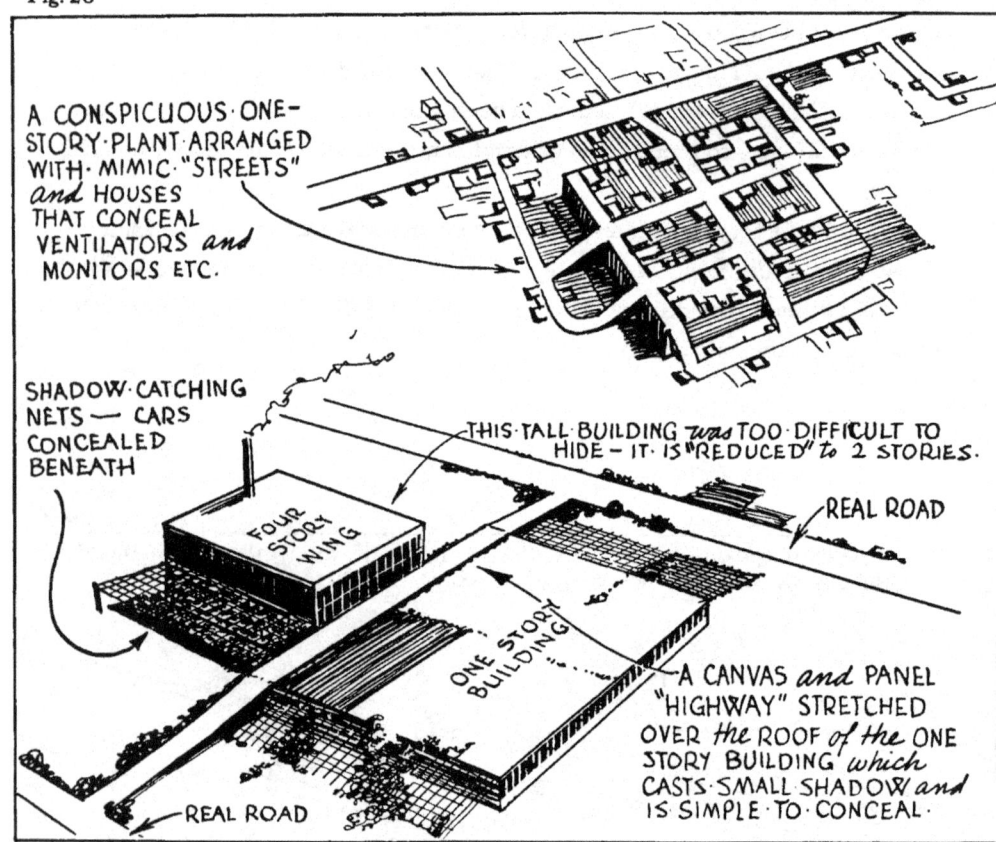

# MIMICRY VERSUS THE BOMBER

## 15

Instruments guide a hostile plane to the attack area but the actual bombing of an objective must depend upon visual aim. Flying at 20,000 feet or more, the bombardier is a busy man. He starts looking for his objective when five and a half miles away. At such an altitude he must drop his load while he is still about two and a half miles from his target. This gives him only about 36 seconds to locate his objective in the bombsight. If there is confusion caused by mimicry, camouflage or blackout, these 36 seconds will be poorly spent and the aim bad.

(Fig. 27) gives a rough idea of what an attacking plane's routine might be. It is easy to see how blacked out towns along the flight path would cause a slight inconvenience. Mimic towns partially blacked out would really confuse the attacker.

Fig. 27

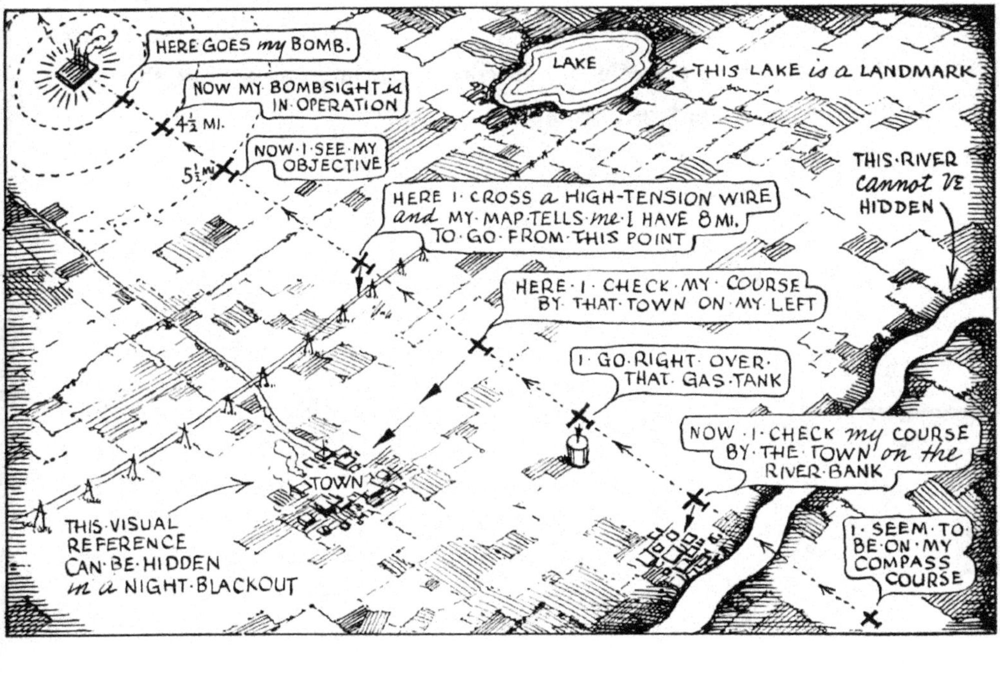

HERE GOES my BOMB.

NOW MY BOMBSIGHT is IN OPERATION

4½ MI.

NOW·I·SEE·MY OBJECTIVE

5½ MI.

LAKE

←THIS LAKE is a LANDMARK

THIS·RIVER cannot be HIDDEN

HERE I CROSS a HIGH-TENSION WIRE and MY·MAP·TELLS·me·I HAVE 8 MI. TO·GO·FROM·THIS POINT

HERE·I·CHECK·MY·COURSE BY THAT·TOWN ON MY LEFT

I·GO·RIGHT·OVER· THAT·GAS·TANK

NOW·I·CHECK my COURSE BY·THE·TOWN on the RIVER·BANK

TOWN

THIS·VISUAL REFERENCE CAN·BE·HIDDEN in a NIGHT·BLACKOUT

I·SEEM·TO· BE·ON·MY COMPASS COURSE

# A B O U T   S M O K E

## 16

The use of smoke for protective concealment is by no means a new idea. Smoke will conceal objects from ground observation, as in the case of the destroyer laying a smoke screen around a battleship. But in aerial observation smoke would be the first thing to call attention to such a target.

White smoke is particularly visible from the air, but dark or colored smoke has good concealment qualities and is more difficult to spot from aloft.

Where factories or installations are located on rivers, lakes or railroad lines, and their concealment is almost impossible, smoke can at least confuse enemy attack. Details of this method of camouflage can be obtained from the Chemical Warfare Service of the U. S. Army.

Existing factory smoke is a great source of worry to the camoufleur. If the smoke is whitish it can be seen even at night. Through the use of certain dyes and acids, black, green, brown, yellow and other color smokes can be produced at will. These are effective in concealing large areas, but should be handled only by expert technicians.

# BLACKOUT

## 17

Blackout is night camouflage. Blackout does not always hide a city, for moonlight, or even starlight, will identify a city from airplane height. But blackout can conceal vital areas in a city as well as public gathering places and landmarks.

Here are the specific things blackouts do:

1) Hide positive targets.

2) Eliminate places for indiscriminate bombings (when the bomber is intercepted and finds he must drop his load and flee).

3) Eliminate landmarks and guides to the objective. Notice in (Fig. 28) how these landmarks lead to the objective.

Light-reflecting surfaces are difficult to conceal, especially large concrete areas, runways, glass roof-windows, rivers and lakes. In drawing 4, notice that the distinct outline of Manhattan is still seen, but since specific areas are difficult to locate the blackout does manage to protect it by lessening its visibility.

Fig. 28

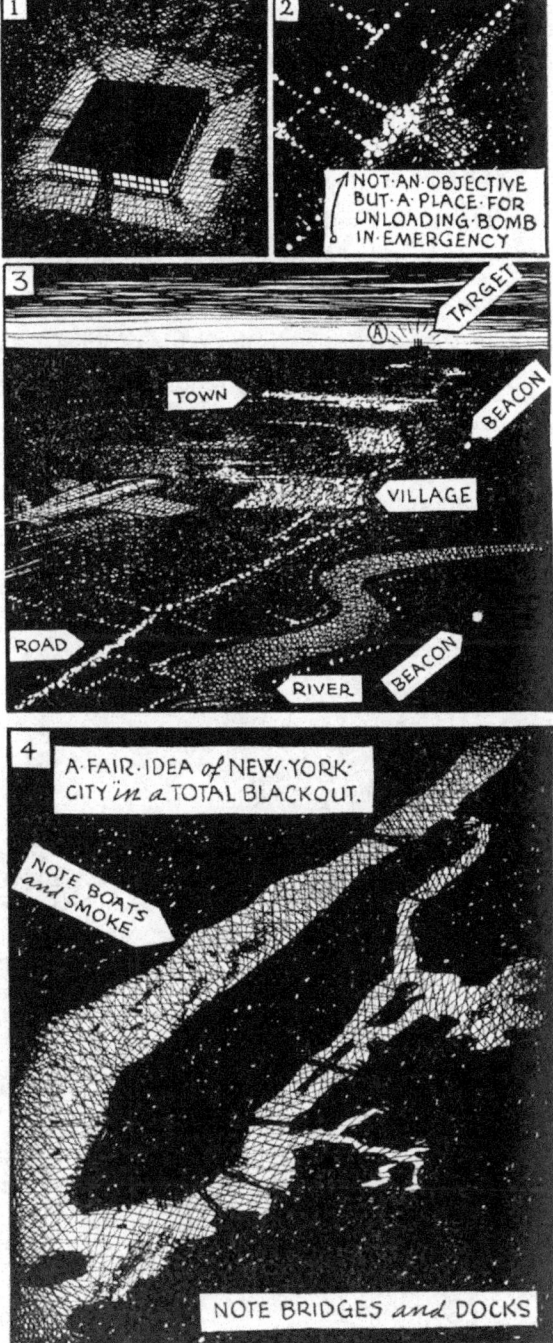

1

2 NOT·AN·OBJECTIVE BUT·A·PLACE·FOR UNLOADING·BOMB IN·EMERGENCY

3 TARGET / A / BEACON / TOWN / VILLAGE / ROAD / RIVER / BEACON

4 A·FAIR·IDEA of NEW·YORK· CITY in a TOTAL BLACKOUT.

NOTE BOATS and SMOKE

NOTE BRIDGES and DOCKS

Blackout equipment, like other camouflage material, is designed for specific requirements. (Fig. 29) shows some of the more generally used methods of blacking out. Asphalt paint (any bituminous emulsion) with sacking cloth pressed into it gives fairly good results. Splinter-proof material is best for smaller windows. Opaque screens must overlap the window and fit snugly. It is advisable to paint a black band of about six inches on the glass around the border of the window to insure against light leakage. Where large factory windows are placed in ceilings, a galvanized beaded tray that can be swung or slid over a window, will not only obscure it, but catch glass that may splinter during a bombing.

The U. S. Office of Civilian Defense has issued a booklet called *Blackouts* containing good plans for industrial blackout provisions. It should be studied.

The simplest method of effecting blackout is to paint the windows black. If the inner sides are painted, the outer sides remain shiny and will reflect sun-

Fig. 29

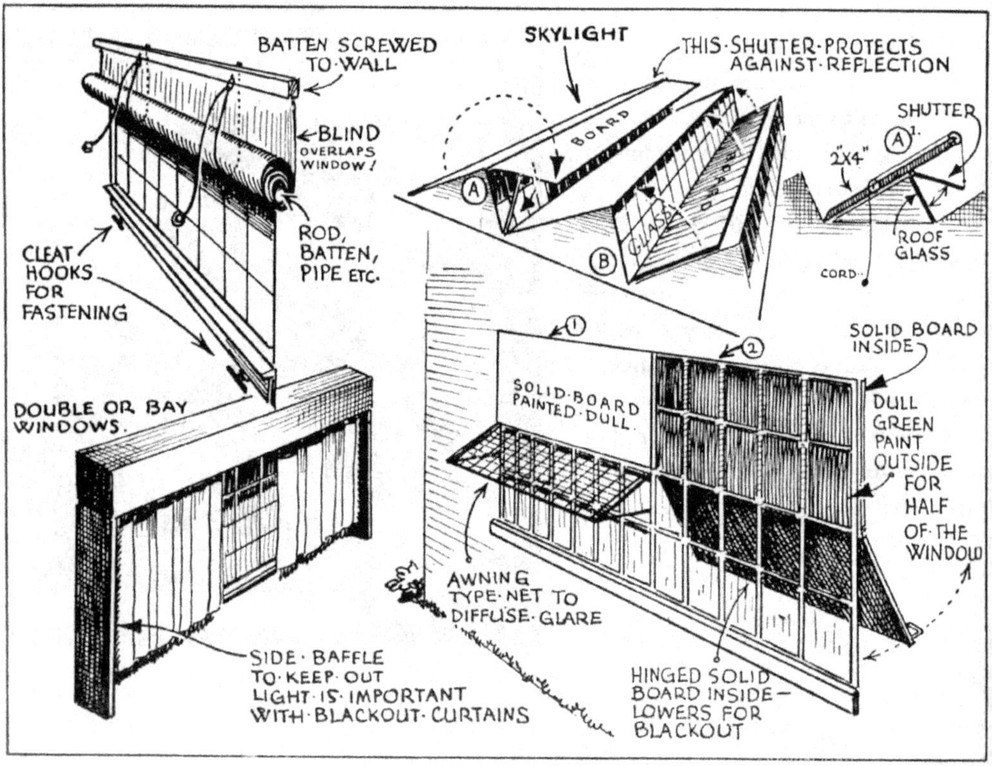

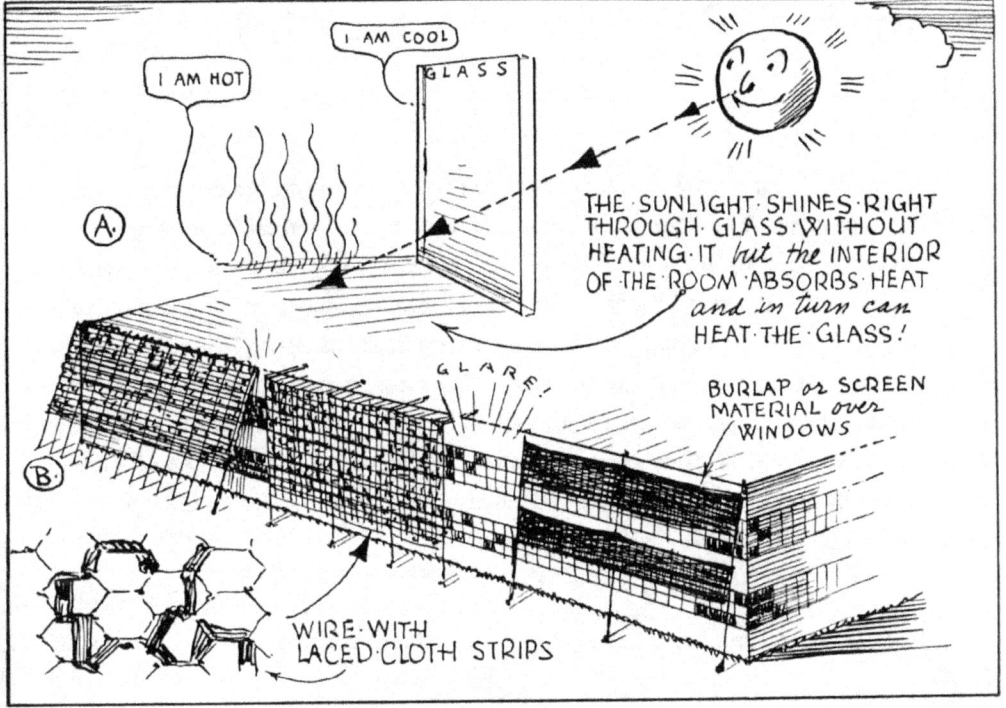

Fig. 30

light, moonlight and starlight. Therefore it is always better to paint the *exposed* surface of the glass.

Window painting however, is not ideal for industrial plants. It fails to make the windows shatter proof; it is difficult to remove; and unlike clear glass, it absorbs the sun's heat (A) (Fig. 30), overheating the interior and often cracking the glass itself. Wherever possible, a protective layer of material which can provide fragmentation protection, as well as blackout, is recommended. Where this is not possible, outer nets (B) (Fig. 30) are a means of reducing window glare caused by sun reflection. Note that direct glare can only be seen in windows with northern exposure at sunset. Solutions to the problem of reflection, as in the case of most other camouflage problems, can best be determined by means of aerial research at different hours of the day.

# THE PROTECTIVE BLANKET
## 18

So-called "blast mattresses" have been made from metal wool similar to sleeping mattresses. They can be hung on brackets outside valuable or dangerous windows. Making these mattresses has cost from 95¢ to $1.60 per square foot, but wartime restrictions on the use of metal discourage their general use. Adjustable curtains lined with thick animal hair matting can be used instead and are attractive to look at. America has pioneered in the use of animal hair matting, which is manufactured already stitched to wire and ready for applying to windows. It offers good protection against bomb fragments and glass splinters. In addition, it blacks out, even if the window shatters, keeps out weather and insulates the building. (Fig. 31).

Fig. 31

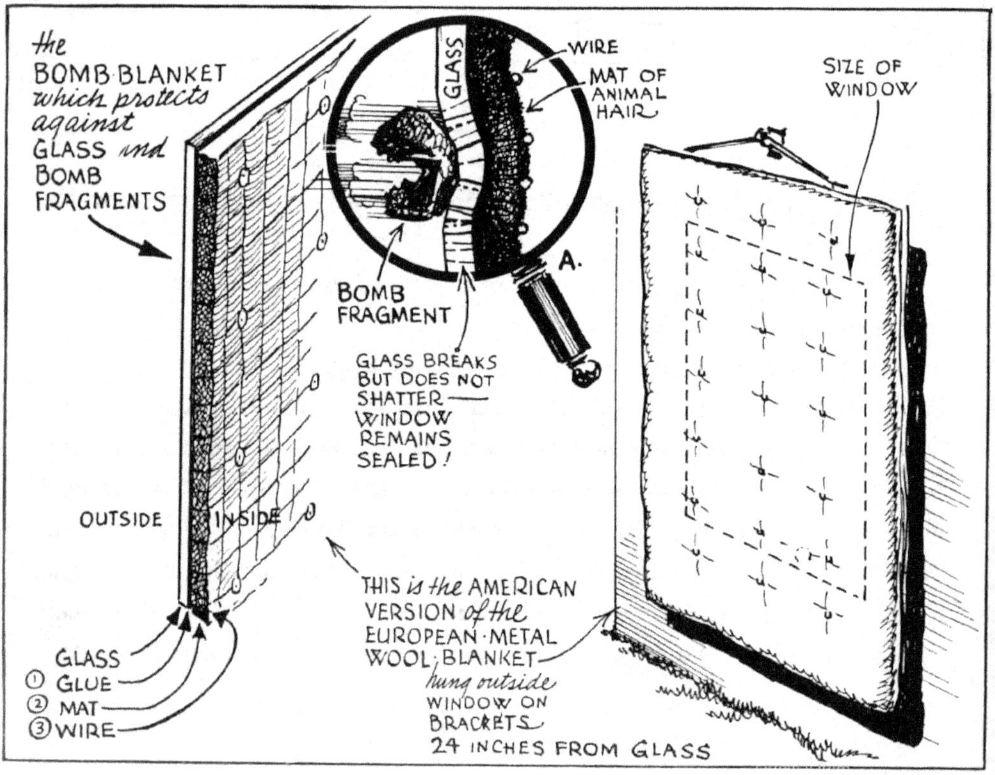

the BOMB·BLANKET which protects against GLASS and BOMB FRAGMENTS

WIRE
MAT OF ANIMAL HAIR
GLASS

SIZE OF WINDOW

A.

BOMB FRAGMENT

GLASS BREAKS BUT DOES NOT SHATTER — WINDOW REMAINS SEALED!

OUTSIDE    INSIDE

THIS is the AMERICAN VERSION of the EUROPEAN·METAL WOOL;BLANKET hung outside WINDOW ON BRACKETS 24 INCHES FROM GLASS

GLASS
① GLUE
② MAT
③ WIRE

# THE USE OF SANDBAGS
## 19

Sandbags have been used in floods and war emergencies for many years. There seems to be no good substitute for the sandbag as an inexpensive and lasting barricade. Where bags are in contact with excessive moisture however, the burlap will rot. San Francisco has perfected a plan for making a more permanent barricade by using 3% by weight of 60 penetration paving asphalt with hot sand, about 250 deg. F., filling bags at the site of the barricade. This mixture hardens to the consistency of soft sandstone and will retain its shape after the bags have rotted away. For simplicity in mixing use 970 pounds of sand and 30 pounds of asphalt. About 160 pounds of mix should be right for each sack. Sacks should be filled only 60% to leave room for molding and tamping.

Fig. 32

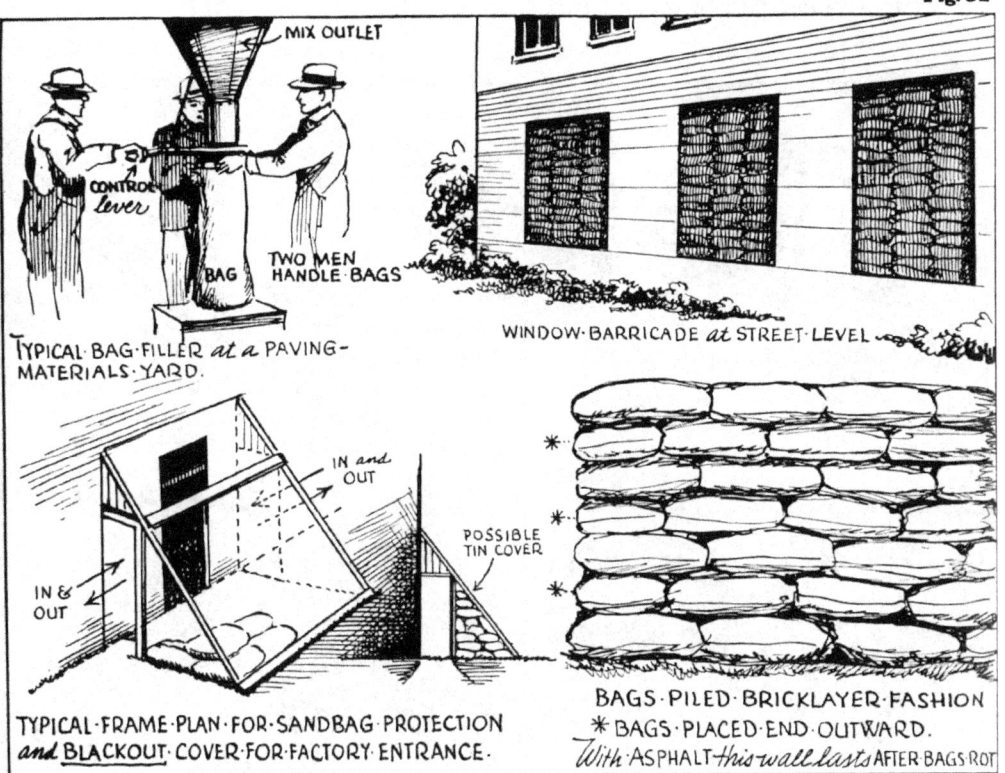

TYPICAL·BAG·FILLER *at a* PAVING-MATERIALS·YARD.

WINDOW·BARRICADE *at* STREET·LEVEL

TYPICAL·FRAME·PLAN·FOR·SANDBAG·PROTECTION *and* BLACKOUT·COVER·FOR·FACTORY·ENTRANCE·

BAGS·PILED·BRICKLAYER·FASHION
* BAGS·PLACED·END·OUTWARD.
*With* ASPHALT *this wall lasts* AFTER·BAGS·ROT

# THE AUTOMOBILE
## 20

A great industrial center may be successful in concealing itself to look like a peaceful farmland, but an area (sometimes larger than the factory itself) filled with workers' automobiles will fairly shriek, *Here are thousands of men at work!* No instrument could be designed to ruin camouflage better than the automobile; parked in geometrical rows, casting sharp shadows, with glass at many angles, they sparkle like black diamonds in sunlight, moonlight or even starlight. Unfortunately, the very effective disrupted parking plan (Fig. 33) with trees for cover, is not popular with many factory workers. A more convenient solution is a net-roofed parking area (C) with woven wire "grass" or other materials. Workers are urged to use fewer cars or to park at a distance from the factory. Where few cars are present, they can be placed under shadow nets or other camouflage material.

Fig. 33

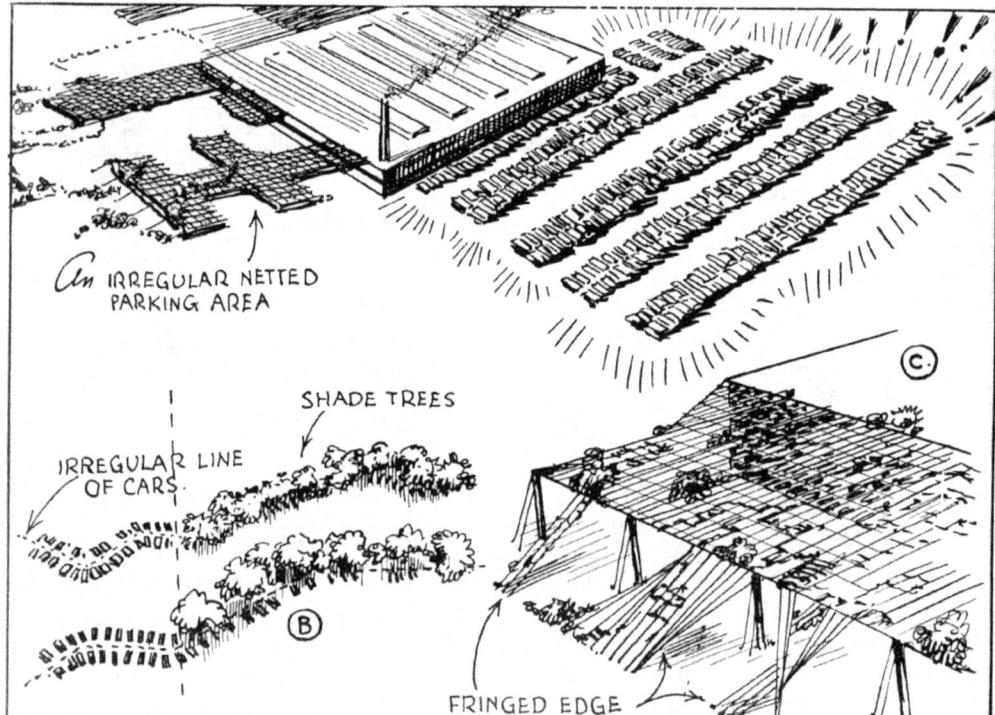

An IRREGULAR NETTED PARKING AREA

SHADE TREES

IRREGULAR LINE OF CARS

Ⓑ

Ⓒ

FRINGED EDGE

# CONCEALMENT PLANTING

## 21

We have remarked that perhaps the peacetime architect of the future will incorporate the concealment factor in his industrial plans and thereby make conversion simpler and less costly when war comes; and the following suggestions are offered for times of peace as well as war in order to make life safer and more attractive for residents of industrial areas.

Factories usually dress their entrances with costly shrubbery and trees for the sake of appearances. Industries near railroads will often display an attractive *front* to the railroad passengers with trees, lawns and even great flower gardens. But because of increasing air travel, the factory of the future will be seen from the air as much as from the ground. Just as camouflage has had to change because of aerial observation, so landscaping will be affected.

Planting is certainly the answer to peacetime concealment, but for hurried wartime problems, the transplanting of trees even large enough to shelter an automobile is difficult and extremely costly. However, for the far sighted and interested industrialist, the following fast growing and tall trees are suggested: Tulip, Chinese Elm, Lombardy Poplar, Cottonwood, the Norway, Red, Box Elder and Sugar varieties of Maple, and White Willow. Although evergreens are hardy and keep their foliage through the winter, they are seldom sheltering and are usually slow growing.

Trees can be utilized in emergency; the plan of draping light rope or net with cloth disruption patterns is a good one. (Fig. 34) (A). This will further cover automobiles that a too small tree would not hide. The point of attachment to the tree should be well covered with soft cloth to allow for wind action and resultant wearing friction.

Drawing (B) shows a factory planting that is so close and even in general texture that the factory shadow has not been disrupted. It is natural that trees and large shrubs planted very close to a factory outline will tend to define that outline, and where a shadow is cast, such foliage will be completely hidden in that shadow. Drawing (C) shows a looser planting which effectively distorts shadows; notice that many of the trees reach above the factory shadow to accomplish this.

But the mere fact of planting trees or shrubs is not enough, and landscaping must be very carefully planned if aerial observation is to be outwitted. Drawing (D) for instance, (Fig. 34) shows how a row of tanks, with trees very high about them, catches shadows and makes them more difficult to see from the air. In wartime this would make painted camouflage more effective. In peacetime, the trees would hide much of the tanks from the ground and also protect them from the sun's heat.

Peacetime concealment has its advantages. Such ugly and massive objects as gas tanks have been treated with concealment patterns for many years, but like early camouflage the general effect has been too colorful, often calling attention rather than diverting. A knowledge of concealment theories will be of use to the architect of the future, hiding industrial sites from neighboring residential communities and doing it with smooth, dignified planting and architectural technique rather than "tricky" painting out, the erection of high walls, etc.

Factories cluttering up an otherwise beautiful water front (and all water fronts are naturally so) will someday be concealed to beautify the community. Such national landmarks as Niagara Falls, New York Harbor and the Mississippi River are fast becoming lost in a maze of gas tanks, power plants, garbage dumps and industrial disposal areas. Here is fertile field for the camoufleur when war ends.

The scheme of grass and tree planting is of the greatest importance to industry. Wild grass seeded into factory lots will grow fast and reduce the dust and heat thereabouts. It also makes the area more presentable to passenger air traffic. Grass is also ideal for the average small airfield, making for softer landings, keener distance judgment for the pilots, and less obvious wheel marks in wartime. Yes, nature if given half a chance, will make our job an easier one, and nature has always been the master camoufleur.

60

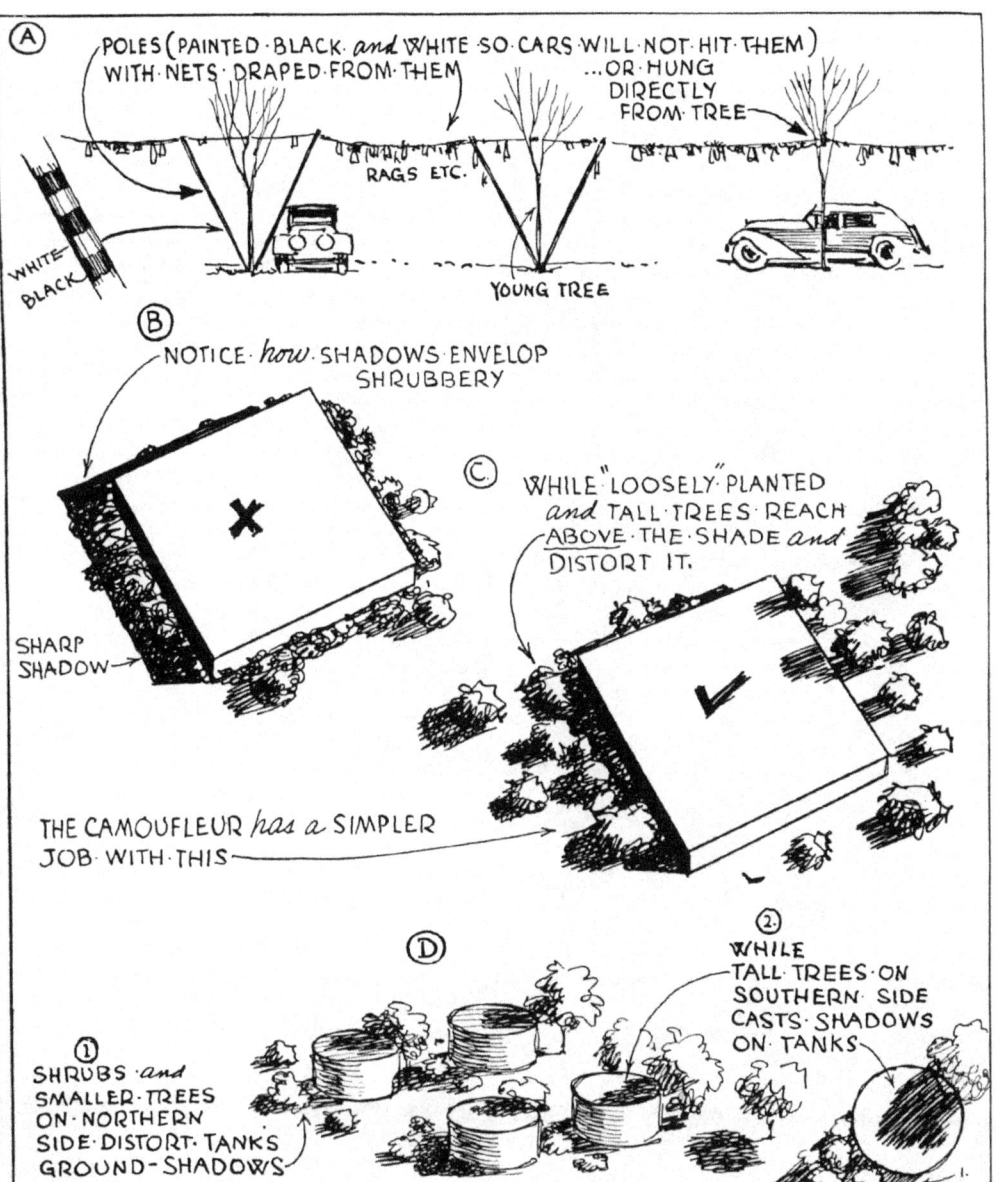

(A) POLES (PAINTED · BLACK *and* WHITE ·SO· CARS ·WILL· NOT· HIT· THEM) WITH · NETS · DRAPED · FROM · THEM

...OR· HUNG DIRECTLY FROM · TREE

RAGS· ETC.

WHITE BLACK

YOUNG· TREE

(B) NOTICE· *how*· SHADOWS· ENVELOP SHRUBBERY

SHARP SHADOW

(C) WHILE "LOOSELY" PLANTED *and* TALL· TREES· REACH ABOVE· THE· SHADE *and* DISTORT· IT.

THE CAMOUFLEUR *has a* SIMPLER JOB· WITH· THIS

(D)

① SHRUBS *and* SMALLER· TREES ON· NORTHERN· SIDE· DISTORT· TANKS GROUND-SHADOWS

② WHILE TALL· TREES· ON SOUTHERN· SIDE CASTS· SHADOWS ON· TANKS

Fig. 34

# BIBLIOGRAPHY

BRECKENRIDGE, LT. COL. R. P., *Modern Camouflage*, Farrar & Rinehart, 1942.

COTT, H. B., *Concealment in Nature*, London.

OFFICE OF CIVILIAN DEFENSE, *Blackouts*, Washington, D. C.

OFFICE OF CIVILIAN DEFENSE, *Protective Concealment*, Washington, D. C.

PRATT INSTITUTE, *Industrial Camouflage*, Reinhold, 1942.

RODYENKO, MAJOR PETER, Articles on Various Phases of Camouflage in *The Military Engineer, Army Ordnance, Marine Corps Gazette, Coast Artillery Journal*, 1940, '41, '42.

WESSMAN, H. E., *Aerial Bombardment Protection*, Wiley, 1942.

CPSIA information can be obtained
at www.ICGtesting.com
Printed in the USA
LVHW081720020919
629671LV00039B/2057/P